Thirty Days With King David

On Leadership

D1128906

Larry Buxton

Front Edge Publishing

For more information and further discussion, visit

www.ThirtyDaysWith.com
www.LarryBuxton.com

Copyright © 2020 by Larry Buxton
All Rights Reserved
ISBN: 978-1-64180-078-5
Version 1.0

Cover design by Rick Nease
www.RickNeaseArt.com

Published by
Front Edge Publishing, LLC
42807 Ford Road, #234
Canton, Michigan

Front Edge Publishing specializes in speed and flexibility in adapting and updating our books. We can include links to video and other online media. We offer discounts on bulk purchases for special events, corporate training, and small groups. We are able to customize bulk orders by adding corporate or event logos on the cover and we can include additional pages inside describing your event or corporation. For more information about our fast and flexible publishing or permission to use our materials, please contact Front Edge Publishing at info@ FrontEdgePublishing.com.

I dedicate this book to everyone who believes that the character of any leader is of critical importance to our nation, our institutions, our congregations and our homes; and to all those who seek to let God shape their character as more virtuous human beings, that their influence may spread to heal our world.

Contents

Praise for
Thirty Days With King David

This engaging study and devotional book based on the biblical story of David ought to be on everyone's list for group study or personal inspiration. Using the lens of the classical theological virtues, Larry Buxton focuses on David as a model for leadership in church and society that allows us to learn from David's admirable qualities, and his glaring failures, as the "man after God's own heart." Buxton is a learned guide, making this *Thirty Days* journey a rich experience of David's life—along with reflections on the virtues needed for effective leadership in our time.

Bruce C. Birch, *Dean Emeritus, Wesley Theological Seminary, Professor Emeritus of Biblical Theology*

For those seeking to read the life of King David through a Christian lens and to extract lessons of leadership therein, *Thirty Days With King David* is accessible and entertaining. Larry Buxton weaves elements of popular culture, political history, and modern management theory into this ancient story.

Rabbi Amy J. Sapowith, *Beth Chaverim Reform Congregation, Ashburn, VA*

As an Imam, I have had the honor of learning from Larry Buxton. He has a unique ability to approach ancient scripture and make it alive and applicable in the modern age. Buxton's insights cross religious lines of demarcation and provide universal insights. In this book, Buxton eloquently points out the traits of true leadership in Prophet Dawud (peace be upon him) as a guidance for Muslims and non-Muslims alike. I am thankful to count him among my colleagues and dear friends.

Imam Mehmet Ayaz, Executive Director of Institute of Islamic Studies and Imam at Ezher Bloom Mosque, Chantilly, VA

This slim volume is rooted in a nuanced, sophisticated understanding of contemporary biblical studies, pastoral care and the complex challenges that leaders must wrestle with on a daily basis in the "Secular City." Larry Buxton reveals himself as a wise listener and questioner, someone who is familiar with what is required of leaders in both family and organizational contexts—a mature, well-differentiated man of faith with something substantive to say in every chapter. I loved how Buxton grounds the entire book within the narrative of David's spiritual journey, respecting both the limits and the richness of solid scriptural scholarship. He helps readers to identify with the universal human joys and sorrows, tragedies and triumphs, that make David's story a template for any leader interested in a more self-aware, reflective life.

It might seem like quite a stretch to use the life of a man dead for three millennia as an entrée into the challenges of 21st-century organizational leadership. But, because the author has avoided portraying David in mythic terms, and because Buxton is obviously familiar with—and at ease with—the real-world problems faced by leaders both at home and at work, the connections he makes between David's journey and the challenges of contemporary leaders flow naturally.

There's no far stretch of the imagination required. This is an easy book to read and to use. The author is plain-spoken; he writes in a very straightforward style, with clarity and without needless rhetorical flourishes. Each chapter engages from the first paragraph, and there is always a nugget—or rather—there is always a substantive take on the challenge of leadership today, followed by thoughtful questions that invite readers to go deeper. Such a format could easily remain on a superficial level, but Buxton manages to nudge the reader to take seriously the invitation to a more reflective engagement, a more mature self-awareness, a more honest look in the mirror.

This is a perfect choice, if you're looking for a very unassuming little book with bite-sized chapters to enjoy for a month—and if you're open to it taking you to a place that will leave you more aware of God's call in your life.

Bob Duggan, *author of* Resilient Leadership *and* Resilient Leadership 2.0

We are navigating through a period that calls for exceptional leadership. This book is a fascinating guide that brings King David's story to the help of contemporary individuals trying to achieve a virtuous life rewarded with success. Larry Buxton seamlessly connects landmark scenes from the King's life with challenges that test the contemporary individual's leadership qualities. This is a timely journey in the footsteps of King David, particularly for those in search for renewed determination to face their own Goliaths, whatever they might be.

It takes exceptional souls to accommodate valor and humility, power and virtue, harp and sword, prudence and courage, determination and openness. King David is certainly one such soul, and this book is a fascinating rediscovery of his landmark legacy of leadership. The life of King David is a constellation of lessons for all those dealing with leadership challenges. Hardly any other perspective will capture the profound relevance of this story for our society better than Buxton's decades-long experience in executing and teaching leadership.

Ibrahim Anli, *Executive Director, Rumi Forum, Washington, DC*

Larry Buxton gives the reader a wide array of readable material on the substantive subjects of the complex King David, the virtues to which all religious people of good will aspire, and what all this means for leadership. Your 30 days with this book will be well-spent.

The Rev. Lovett H. Weems, Jr., *Distinguished Professor of Church Leadership Emeritus, Wesley Theological Seminary, Washington, DC*

There is no better example for leadership in the bible than King David. We don't know enough intimate narrative details about Abraham, Moses or Joseph, or even Peter. Paul is more like a consultant. We can't really lead like Jesus—Him, we follow as Christians. But we can lead like David. Or, at least, we can learn from David's leadership. And, we can identify with him. I can, anyway, and not just because I am his namesake. It's because of his flaws as much as his virtues. We see him both dance with joy and cower in shame.

The useful takeaways are the elements of his character as a leader. This is the value of *Thirty Days With King David* for those aspiring or struggling to be in positions of leadership. Larry Buxton draws from both his study of the classical virtue ethics and his many years as a successful pastor to look at David with critical appreciation. Larry has paid attention to what leadership requires in himself and the many leaders he has known.

We are a faith founded in the life and ministry of the one "born in the city of David." Our tradition, and the congregations and institutions within it, are based on the incarnation—meaning, it is not otherworldly, it's earthy. That means: It is worth studying this book. King David is a real character. We can walk around him, like we would Michelangelo's statue, and see the good side and bad side of being a leader.

David McAllister-Wilson, *President, Wesley Theological Seminary*

Foreword

By U.S. Sen. Timothy Kaine

Why is the Bible the most read book in human history? Of course, the main reason is Jesus, the "luminous Nazarene" in the words of Albert Einstein. But another reason is surely the number of fascinating characters who populate its pages.

Some are memorable even though they appear briefly. Who can forget Nathanael of Cana, hearing of a Messiah, and sarcastically asking "Can anything good come out of Nazareth?" There's the unforgettable Lazarus, the brother of Mary and Martha, described as one of Jesus's close friends—whose death causes Jesus to cry. Lazarus's resurrection is both one of Jesus's major miracles and the last straw leading to his crucifixion—yet, Lazarus appears in just two scenes and never speaks a word. Millions around the world also recall the unnamed Samaritan woman at the well whose one interaction with Jesus touches upon his divinity, the nature of discipleship, forgiveness and the prejudices of the day. And these three vivid supporting players are examples from just one of the Bible's many books—the Gospel of John!

Many other characters—Jesus, of course, and also Peter, Paul, Moses, Job, Ruth—are fleshed out in deep detail as if in a great novel. Their characters are full of the motivations, achievements, failures and contradictions that are common, or at least recognizable, to us all. One of those fully realized characters is the great leader of the people Israel, King David.

In the earlier *Thirty Days with Abraham Lincoln*, Lincoln scholar Duncan Newcomer distilled dozens of leadership lessons from the life of our greatest American president. Now, the Rev. Dr. Larry Buxton presents life lessons from another towering figure we all revere: King David, who united the nation of Israel 1,000 years before Christ's birth.

David is an interesting—and controversial—choice to follow Lincoln in this series. When Larry Buxton tells a parishioner about this writing project, she responds by recounting King David's rape of Bathsheba and his scheming to get Bathsheba's husband Uriah killed in battle—and labels David a "sleazeball."

Of course, there's so much more to this story! Just as the prophet Samuel saw something in this youngest son of Jesse, and King Saul asked the humble shepherd boy to come be his right hand, Larry Buxton sees 30 days of valuable lessons in David. Chief among those lessons that cross thousands of years is that even a "sleazeball"—we might call him "a flawed human being"—can be used by God for a mighty purpose.

What a complex life to analyze! David was plucked from obscurity, led the Israelites to victory over Goliath and the Philistines in one of history's paradigmatic battles, became a King that unified tribes into the nation of Israel, earned admiration as a skillful musician and wrote portions of The Book of Psalms, one of the world's best-known literary works. But, this was not a life of untrammeled success or consistent virtue. In addition to his grotesque scheme to entice Bathsheba and arrange for her husband's death, he had a prickly temper, was prone to exaggerated self-importance, labored in an often unhappy marriage to King Saul's daughter Michal, had to confront incest and murder among his many children and was even forced to defend his kingdom from a lengthy insurrection led by his own son Absalom. Thankfully, David did possess the rare trait, much like Peter, of being able to see when he was wrong and then sincerely admit and atone for his sins. This trait came in handy and was much used during his life.

From the blockbuster arc of David's life, Larry Buxton assembles 30 short chapters on key leadership traits—patience, vision, humility, integrity, openness, tenderness, forgiveness, courage, gratitude, self-control, surrender, perseverance, calmness, justice. Buxton helps us see how David either exhibited these values or catastrophically failed to achieve them. The chapters are probing and conversational—with references from the worlds of literature, sports, politics and entertainment to illustrate how to apply these lessons to our everyday challenges.

A personal favorite is humility, which is not thinking less of yourself—but thinking of yourself less.

And the book is not only geared toward personal introspection, but also includes materials to enhance group discussion and activities to bring the wisdom to life.

I have a son who is an infantry officer in the Marines, and he tells me about his own leadership training: "Dad, I've served under a lot of officers and I learn just as much from the bad ones as the good ones." King David was a good one *and* a bad one, just as most of us are.

While David's highs were higher than most, and his lows lower than most, there is much to gain by spending time with this groundbreaking leader. He lived more than 3,000 years ago, but the basics of human nature have not changed much in that span. Or, in the words of my second favorite president, Harry Truman, "the only thing new in the world is the history you don't know."

Summer, 2020

Timothy Michael Kaine is the U.S. Senator from Virginia. An attorney and educator, Kaine has served as an elected leader at local, state and national levels since 1994. In the 1990s, he was mayor of Richmond; in 2005, he was elected Governor of Virginia; in 2016, he was Hillary Clinton's vice-presidential running mate; then, in 2018, he was re-elected to the U.S. Senate.

Preface

By Andrew H. Card, Jr.

When Adam and Eve were given life by God—God also included the remarkable gift of free choice and with it came the responsibility of leadership.

Oh, how that reality has impacted all human life!

The Rev. Dr. Larry Buxton, with meticulous biblical research, takes this divinely designated leader from his teenage anointing, through his training and tests of leadership and then his 33 years of reign as king. As we read through these 30 days, we experience along with David all of the challenges, temptations, palace intrigue, egos, frustrations, failures and successes and even abandonment. The wisdom in these pages is more than a history lesson or a Bible Study. Truly, these 30 reflections on David's life become for us a timeless guide to understanding the responsibilities and consequences of leadership.

No matter what your faith or tradition of worship—and, no matter your role in business, management, philanthropy, sports, politics, government or family—you will find the adventures in these 30 daily readings extremely relevant and highly motivating. We need to meet David again through Larry Buxton's wise retelling of these stories—so that we all can lift up the best values in leadership in our institutions, our nation and our world.

Over the course of my life, I have been blessed to work for and with remarkable leaders. In business, as a structural design engineer; in government, at the local level and as a member of the Massachusetts House of Representatives; and in many roles for three U. S. presidents. I served twice a Member of the Cabinet, once as Secretary of Transportation and then as White House Chief of Staff under President George W. Bush. For several years, I was president of a trade association representing the captains of the American Automobile Manufacturers: GM, Ford and Chrysler. Later, I was a vice president of General Motors. In education, I served as a dean at Texas A&M University and more recently as president of Franklin Pierce University. Additionally, I have served in many roles for not-for-profit institutions, and am currently chair of the National Endowment for Democracy.

So many experiences in so many different kinds of organizations taught me that effective leadership rests on a solid foundation of values.

In these pages, Larry Buxton offers us an in-depth journey through the many turbulent twists and turns of David's long career—as he had to struggle repeatedly to grasp that sure foundation. In my own journey through this book, I found myself recalling and reflecting on the wisdom of leaders who led me. I kept asking myself: How can I be a better leader going forward?

If you aspire to be a leader: read this book. It is a road map that will help to form your conscience.

If you are a leader: read this book. It will have you reflecting on how you accepted and responded to that challenge—and will leave you better able to meet the challenges ahead.

If you are teaching leaders: read this book. You will have new context to help form and launch the leaders of character we so urgently need to send into our world today.

Summer, 2020

Andrew Hill Card, Jr. has been a leader in the U.S. auto industry, a top figure in Washington D.C. and an educator. Among his many roles, he served as U.S. Secretary of Transportation under President George H. W. Bush and was Chief of Staff under President George W. Bush from 2001 to 2006. He also was president of Franklin Pierce University in New Hampshire until his retirement in 2016.

Introduction:
David and the
Cardinal Virtues

David is the world's most popular writer.

How can that be, in this era of mega-bestsellers like the *Harry Potter* series? First, consider that billions of people around the world know at least a few of David's best lines by heart, including the timeless 23rd psalm: *"The Lord is my shepherd; I shall not want. He makes me lie down in green pastures."* The Book of Psalms, a collection of ancient hymns, is the most popular book in the Bible, according to the latest polling data. In fact, the Bible still ranks as the world's all-time bestseller, with more than 4 billion copies published. The Quran, which features David as a major prophet, ranks second.

Why is David's poetry still so popular? C.S. Lewis put it simply: "The most valuable thing the Psalms do for me is to express the same delight in God that made David dance."

The flawed and heroic life of David is a mirror for our souls, as Scriptures have reminded us for thousands of years. The Gospel of Matthew calls Jesus "the son of David," Christmas stories place Jesus' birth in David's city of Bethlehem, and Christian writers chart many other connections between David and his descendant. In Islam, David appears repeatedly in the Quran as a prophet and messenger of God, and as a divinely anointed king. Muslims honor David for having received divine revelation of the Psalms.

David also is a superhero in an age when superheroes are ascending in our global culture. David became a king through events that seem torn from the pages of a comic book. In fact, there are now dozens of graphic novels that tell his story.

These are the reasons that countless writers now look to David as a universal example of leadership. Journalist Malcolm Gladwell chose David as his title hero for the bestseller *David and Goliath: Underdogs, Misfits, and the Art of Battling Giants.* Dozens of other books have explored David's life and legacy and include lessons on prayer, conflict, music, failure, repentance, spirituality, leadership, history, worship, sexuality, administration and ethics. That list of books quickly becomes thousands of titles if we add in all of the religious books involving David that have been produced through the centuries for pastors, Sunday schools and other congregational study groups.

King David and Abraham Lincoln

In this second volume in our *30 Days With* series, we move from Abraham Lincoln—who we described as "the soul of America," in our first volume—to a truly global soul. Like Lincoln, David was called to leadership in a turbulent era of war. As with Lincoln, library shelves groan with all the volumes exploring David's life. Yet the wisdom we can glean from David's life still is sorely needed, in this era when so many Goliaths are rising around the world.

Like Lincoln, David is a symbol of unity. In Judaism, David plays a central role in the story of liberation and the elevation of Jerusalem as the geographic center of the faith. Thousands of years later, observant Jews recite David's psalms as part of their daily prayers. Muslims honor David as well.

David and Abraham Lincoln also share the distinction of having triumphed despite agonizing flaws and shortcomings. That's a comparison Rabbi David Wolpe makes in the opening pages of his classic, *David: The Divided Heart.* After comparing the allure of David's life story to Lincoln's, Rabbi Wolpe writes:

Other ancient figures have stories, powerful ones; but they are fragments of character, marked by tendentiousness and heavy symbolism. David is the first person in history whose tale is complete and vital, laced with passions, savagery, hesitation, betrayal, charisma, faith, family—the rich canvas of a large life. He is capable of great acts, expressions of lasting piety, and of startling cruelty. David's failings are not slight or endearing. Whitman famously said of himself that he contained multitudes. Long before Whitman, the Bible's premier poet had a soul so large that thousands of years of interpretation have not exhausted its landmarks and byways.

I agree with the rabbi. Throughout my own life, I've been struck by how the very flaws and tragedies in David's life forged the leader he became. This is an often messy and sometimes bloody story. We don't observe David confidently doling out his "seven habits" or "five techniques" or "three keys" to success. Instead, we read stories of a young man growing into maturity, doing some things well and other things poorly. David brings himself—good and bad, wise and foolish—into God's presence. God uses David's flawed life and evolving character to lead the nation of Israel into its golden age.

A Daily Tool for Growth of Character

Delving deeper into these stories can provide us with new perspectives to recognize and wider insights to nurture. Stories of David illuminate some of the rich and diverse ways God works in human life. Reflecting on these stories begins to shape us from the inside out. When we read, ponder, discuss, ask, listen, pray and act, we develop our own character in the light of God.

This book is a daily tool for doing just that. It's a means of character formation, in sync with Paul's encouraging his Roman church: "Do not conform to the pattern of this world, but be transformed by the renewing of your mind. Then you will be able to test and approve what God's will is—his good, pleasing and perfect will." (Romans 12:2)

A well-informed mind can bring clarity to our prayer and our development. God will encourage us as we test and welcome his fullest presence within.

This is a timely message in a deeply troubled century. Seeking God's presence is one of the great, restless quests of our age. Spending time exploring the Bible's deep wisdom is especially important because of a uniquely American dilemma: The vast majority of Americans tell pollsters year after year that they love the Bible, but the depth of Americans' understanding of the text has grown paper-thin and fragile in recent decades. Here's one of the most telling examples: The vast majority of Americans tell pollsters they own a Bible, and more than half say they regularly read it. Everyone says they know the Bible. Then, if pollsters ask a person to simply name the four Gospels, less than half can recall Matthew, Mark, Luke and John.

What does "everyone know" about King David? He killed Goliath. He left us many psalms. Michelangelo thought he was an ideal model of a man. Beyond those world-famous reference points, how can we describe such an idealized life? How can we hope to measure such an oversized figure? How can we hope to find lessons that can apply to our ordinary lives thousands of years after David walked his corner of the earth?

The Cardinal Virtues in Daily Life

In the Western and Christian traditions, the classic way to consider moral character has been through the "cardinal virtues." The term cardinal comes from the Latin word *cardo* (hinge). They are the basic or fundamental virtues required for a life of high character. Philosophers as far back as Plato and Cicero wrote about them; St. Paul quoted several lists of virtues in his letters; and St. Thomas Aquinas did a detailed, systematic reflection on these virtues in his classic *Summa Theologica*. So, welcome to an impressive line of scholars and thinkers! In these pages, we will ponder some of the very same matters.

The four Cardinal Virtues are historically understood to be:

- Prudence (deciding well, assessing and choosing wisely)
- Courage (confronting obstacles, pursuing the good with steadfastness)

- Temperance (seeking harmony, moderating desires and appetites)
- Justice (treating people fairly, living in right relationship with others)

As we look at David's life, multiple virtues will shine through. Each virtue is necessary to reinforce the others. I link a dimension of each virtue to an event that reveals David's character as a leader. I use everyday names to expand the meaning of each one. For example:

- Humility, openness and gratitude are aspects of Prudence.
- Perseverance, patience, vision, and surrender (repentance) are aspects of Courage.
- Self-control, calmness, and tenderness are aspects of Temperance.
- Forgiveness and integrity are aspects of Justice.

These words are our signposts in this month-long journey. Each day, we will take another step through the epic of David's life. Some days we will delve deeply into a key event in his life; other days we will reflect on different writers and teachers who have pondered these same events and trials. Each day's reading begins with a brief, relevant quote from Scripture, plus a reference to a longer passage you can read for added context to that day's challenge.

Resources for Individuals and Group Discussion

After the 30 daily readings, the book concludes with additional ideas and resources for expanding on this inspiring adventure among your friends and community. You will also find a link to the online resource page for this book, along with all of the *30 Days With* books. The *30 Days With* resource pages offer everything from voices of reviewers and readers to study guides and news about upcoming publications.

Have fun as you reflect on fresh connections drawn between these stories, the wisdom you find in Scripture and new ways to connect these values with our contemporary world. As you see the overall pattern of David's moral character emerge, along with his sometimes-hard-earned lessons in leadership, you may want to talk about these insights with friends. This book is ideal for individual reading, as well as for sparking discussion in classes, small groups or circles of friends.

The *30 Days With* books already are sparking new kinds of national conversations that gather people together around values and stories we all share, despite the differences that are so visible in front-page news stories each day. When the first volume about Abraham Lincoln was released in late 2019, for example, a Sunday column by *The Christian Science Monitor* editor Mark Sappenfield called on all Americans to read along.

Now, in this second volume, I thank you for joining me—and so many other readers—in sharing David's dramatic life. Thank you for entering this national conversation and showing that we all have much to share in our communities.

Whether you use this as a personal resource or in a small group, I hope you find that it fosters spiritual growth.

The path before you these next 30 days truly is an adventure. For thousands of years, these timeless stories have inspired and transformed lives.

Now, it's your turn.

Welcome to our community.

May God bless you richly in the days ahead.

—Larry Buxton and the Front Edge Publishing team, 2020

Patience

Prepare the Way of the King

The Lord said to Samuel, "The Lord does not see as mortals see; they look on the outward appearance, but the Lord looks on the heart." Then Samuel took the horn of oil, and anointed David in the presence of his brothers.

Highlights from 1 Samuel 16:1-13

WHY DO MILLIONS of people flock to Florence every year to join a long line, waiting to gaze at Michelangelo's statue of David? The answer is quite simple: This towering marble likeness still ignites imaginations and fuels dreams, more than 500 years after it was unveiled.

Who was David? Jews, Christians and Muslims around the world know that he was once a divinely anointed king in Jerusalem. He was the second of three kings to rule over the united kingdom of Israel and Judah, about a thousand years before Jesus was born. David followed the tragic King Saul and was succeeded by his equally famous successor, his son, Solomon. David's reign has often been referred to as the "Golden Age" of Israel.

This royal epic did not begin in the halls of power, however. On the contrary, it began in the rocky fields around Bethlehem, with a boy almost forgotten by his father.

Imagine a time machine that lifts us from the present day, sending us back in time and halfway around the world. For a moment, we're overwhelmed by whooshing noises and dizzying blurs, until finally, the pace begins to slow. We've gone back roughly 3,000 years! We hover over the arid lands of Israel, and we begin to move closer to the ground. A young boy comes into focus, alone in a pasture and far from the nearest building.

This is David. He's a boy, about 12 or 13 years old, and he spends long days watching sheep in his father's pasture. When important things happen at his family's house, he's a long way off. To his father, Jesse, he's practically an afterthought. Easily overlooked and almost forgotten, David barely registers.

The spark that ignites David's story comes in the form of an old man—a royal prophet. This elderly man, named Samuel, plays an important role in both the Bible and the Quran. He has been told by God to select the next king of Israel. While on his journey, he was divinely led to the homestead where David resides.

Samuel approaches Jesse, the father of eight sons. After routine pleasantries, Samuel asks Jesse to line up his boys. Pausing to carefully observe each one, and starting with the oldest, Samuel thinks to himself that each is royal material.

God has other plans, however. As Samuel pauses in front of each son, he gets a divine nudge: No, not this one. No, not this one. No—

Finally, he's at the end.

"Are these all of your boys?" Samuel asks Jesse.

"Well, there's actually one more," mutters Jesse, "but ..."

But what? It's inconvenient to call him? He's just a kid? Someone wouldn't be interested in a boy who does menial labor? Jesse barely advocates for his own son! The overlooked child in each of us winces at this part of the story.

David is young, yes—but he's old enough to see the world around him, to appreciate the activity in the barn or the house, and to grasp the workings of the family business. He's also the eighth of eight. Last in line.

Jesse ultimately summons David. Then, as Samuel stands before David, he finally hears God speak: "This is the one." So Samuel anoints him. Readers are told simply that the Lord's spirit rested on David from that day forward.

What actually happened in that encounter? How did David (and his family) understand Samuel's action? We might assume that Samuel made some explanation to David about what he was doing and what was happening. Being anointed by the nation's prophet, a man renowned as God's emissary, had to signal a unique and powerful future for the young boy.

Samuel and his entourage leave. All too soon David is back in the fields, watching over sheep. Certainly, he is pondering the impact of Samuel's visit at this point. What had it all been about? What would it mean for him? What would happen next? When?

David's first test as a leader, then, is to practice patience. He must learn to let God's future unfold in God's time. He must wait and be alert, think long-term, and trust in God's presence and guidance when nothing visible is pointing toward his unique future.

Leo Tolstoy wrote, "The two most powerful warriors are patience and time." In his earliest years, David has both of these—patience and time—and uses them to prepare for his mission. Likewise, good leaders understand that progress rarely happens quickly. Leadership requires the ability to think and plan long-term.

Throughout my 40-year career as a pastor, consultant and church leader, I have never seen a leadership book begin with a chapter on patience; in fact, just the opposite. A cursory search for leadership books turns up titles such as *The Speed of Trust, Smarter Faster Better, High Output Management, Taking Action*—and, even, *How to Be a Kick-Ass Boss.*

Apparently, impatience rules.

The late economist Milton Friedman famously said that the purpose of a corporation is to maximize profits for shareholders. Following this philosophy, speed and action are highly valued. To be patient is to be left behind. The pressure to succeed drives leaders to chase short-term results that look like victories.

But business experts today are increasingly warning against the effects of fast-paced, high-stress workplaces and profit-focused goals. Business leaders are beginning to realize that, in the long run, these practices frequently cost the organization, its employees and even the surrounding community. The CEO turnover rate is the highest it has been in years. Corporations are paying out multi-billion-dollar settlements for fraud, discrimination and theft.

Effective leaders are learning to discover the value of the long view. In August 2019, the Business Roundtable issued a landmark statement that broadened the purpose of corporations beyond Friedman's long-standing philosophy. Their "Statement on the Purpose of a Corporation" calls for honoring such practices as fair compensation and benefits, adequate training, continuing education, ethical dealing, protection of the environment and the generation of long-term value.

To do this, I'm convinced that leaders will need to revisit Tolstoy's "powerful warrior": patience. Leaders will need the discipline to listen more broadly, reflect more deeply and plan more carefully. Companies will need to begin unlearning their blinded focus on the bottom line and relearning to see more widely.

Think about a time in the past when pressure to act quickly led you to regret a choice. What caused you to act with such haste? Why did patience get no respect in your decision-making?

What enables you to be patient? How do you cultivate patience? What spiritual resources help you stay calm when those around you are in a panic?

What demands are you facing this week that will require your patience?

Your own leadership work might begin as David's work did—with patience.

David Ponders His Future

One of King Saul's young men reported, "I have seen a son of Jesse the Bethlehemite who is skillful in playing, a man of valor, a warrior, prudent in speech, and a man of good presence; and the Lord is with him."

So, Saul sent messengers to Jesse, and said, "Send me your son David who is with the sheep."

David came to Saul and entered his service.

Highlights from 1 Samuel 16:14-23

IN *THE 7 Habits of Highly Effective People* and other books, Stephen Covey teaches the difference between what's urgent and what's important. The two are rarely the same.

Urgency covers all things that demand our attention *now*, Covey explains. While some urgent matters arise unexpectedly, most things in life that are urgent are the result of procrastination. Living in urgency usually results from the failure to act sooner on information already possessed. We've delayed planning, put off starting or neglected to anticipate deadlines. Urgency is frequently marked by short tempers, high anxiety, fear of making mistakes, overlooked details, jumbled responsibilities, blame and more. All of this undermines effectiveness.

Effective leaders, on the other hand, learn to focus on what's truly important. They build over a period of time, in order to anticipate and prepare. Important activities include strategic planning, the building of relationships, a clarification of values, the development of employee skills, reflection, writing and so on. There's rarely an immediate payoff for, say, having coffee and a conversation with a difficult co-worker. Since the payoff is not always immediately obvious, doing what's important requires patience.

Covey's point is that focusing on important work minimizes times of anxious urgency. When deadlines or crises emerge, there's a greater likelihood of smooth cooperation and shared trust if leaders have been focusing on the important work all along. If we begin with patience, we also have time to clarify and act on our fundamental values. We can organize our time in ways that will help us accomplish these values.

Great leaders understand the power of patience, just as Covey stresses. Yet this principle works in our personal lives, too. On a practical level, steadily putting away money helps to avoid panic when the tax bill comes.

There's also a spiritual aspect to this truth. With patience, we have time to appreciate God's role in our lives. In the Bible, "patience" is a recurring description of what God is doing with us. Just a few examples:

- The Apostle Paul summarizes the whole action of God toward us as "the riches of his kindness and forbearance and patience." (Romans 2:4)

- Our very purpose and destiny in life is linked to this quality: "Regard the patience of our Lord as salvation." (2 Peter 3:15)

- When Paul begins to define love in action (1 Corinthians 13), he starts his list this way: "Love is patient …"

- Patience is one of the fruits of the Holy Spirit (Galatians 5:22f.), the behavior we will demonstrate when God's spirit dwells within us.

- Proverbs 19:11 teaches that, even in our ordinary dealings, patience is related to wisdom. "Those with good sense are slow to anger, and it is their glory to overlook an offense."

Perhaps some people are born patient, but the truth is this: Patience doesn't come easily to most of us. I often hear myself muttering, "I just don't have the patience for that." But I have learned that there are ways I can slow down and cultivate this virtue. Timeless spiritual practices—mindfulness, spending time in nature, meditation, slow walking and deep breathing—help us to develop patience. Those who believe that patience comes from God can nurture it by spending time with God through Scripture reading, prayer, worship, singing and sharing with friends.

We know that David spent time with God in worship, prayer, music and Torah reading, and in such he slowly developed his own patient faith. At this point in our story, he's still an adolescent given a clear destiny from God's prophet, but he's years away from being able to get started. Patience is an unusual first step for a leader, but that's precisely what David has to learn first.

Letters to a Young Poet is a classic among writers who admire the poet Rainer Maria Rilke, because it collects a series of letters that he wrote to a young cadet at a military academy who was struggling to discern his vocation. The cadet was so moved by this correspondence that he published the letters in book form after Rilke died in 1926—thereby sharing the poet's wisdom with all of us. In one letter, the cadet had asked Rilke if he had the talent to be a poet. Rilke responded:

> "I want to beg you, as much as I can, dear sir, to be patient toward all that is unsolved in your heart and to try to love the questions themselves, like locked rooms and like books that are written in a very foreign tongue. Do not now seek the answers, which cannot be given you because you would not be able to live them. And the point is, to live everything. Live the questions now. Perhaps you will then gradually, without noticing it, live along some distant day into the answer."

This seems like the advice a mentor might have given to young David—or to any of us wrestling with vocational questions today. What we do know is that David had a long period out in his father's far fields to "love" and "live" such questions, as Rilke put it. Can you imagine what that might have been like for this young boy? While he's shepherding the family flocks, he ponders the "locked rooms" of his destiny. How do you think that David prepares and plans for that destiny?

In the same way, what currently remains "unsolved" in your heart? Is there a dream that you, too, are patiently waiting to pursue? What might God be nudging you toward? How can you learn to "love the questions themselves" as you wait?

On a different level, you might reflect on how you're spending your days. Are you making time for the important work of reflection, planning, learning and building relationships? Or are you living deadline to deadline, overwhelmed? What personal habits or institutional patterns force you to work with urgency and anxiety? In what situations could you nurture and practice more patience?

Vision

David Confronts Goliath

David said to Saul, "Let no one's heart fail because of him;
your servant will go and fight with this Philistine."

Saul said to David, "You are not able to go against this Philistine to fight
with him; for you are just a boy, and he has been a warrior from his youth."

Highlights from 1 Samuel 17:1-58

A FEW YEARS pass in our story. Throughout the area, battles and skirmishes break out repeatedly. During these years, King Saul's mental problems worsen, and he's increasingly in anguish. David is referred to him as a lyre player who can soothe his tormented spirit, and Saul invites David into his royal household. David enters the court as a musician who is also skilled in fighting, and the shepherd boy immediately becomes the royal musician and armor bearer.

Tensions with the neighboring Philistines begin to mount. The Philistines occupy the western, coastal region of Israel, while the Israelites under Saul hold the mountainous, eastern region. The Philistines want to split Saul's kingdom in two and capture Israel's land, so they advance to the Elah River and take up camp at Azekah, on the southern ridge. Israel moves its army to the northern hill, in the region known as Socoh. *(If you are reading other sources, perhaps another translation of the Bible, you may find that the spelling of these ancient names vary.)*

Finally, the two armies face off in a river valley about 12 miles west of Bethlehem. David's three oldest brothers are in the army there, and David travels back and forth between the grazing field and the battlefield with some frequency—and that's no quick trip by foot in that region.

The confrontation is supposed to feature the best warriors of each side: Israel's best against the Philistines' best. The two armies gear up and descend into the valley to taunt and insult each other, but no one does any actual fighting. This is because the Philistines' best warrior, Goliath, totally terrifies the Israelite soldiers. His size, his strength and the fearsomeness of his weapons is chilling. The Israelites have no one comparable to put up against this behemoth.

When Goliath strides forth, Israel runs.

David asks some of the soldiers for an update. In essence, David's oldest brother, Eliab, snaps at his little brother. "What are you doing here, twerp? Who's taking care of the sheep?"

David responds. "Chill out, Eliab! I'm just asking a question. Mind your own business."

The more David learns about Israel's fear of Goliath, the more incensed he becomes. Since he sees Israel as a nation created by God, he reasons that anyone who insults Israel is insulting God. This is intolerable. His questions and mutterings lead Saul to summon David.

As soon as he's in Saul's presence, David blurts out his offer. "I'll go out and fight Goliath!"

Saul chuckles. "You? Ha! You're just a boy!"

Is he? How old is David at this point? There's a lot of conjecture, but here is a good approach to figure out the answer: A man needed to be 20 years old to fight in the army. We know that David is the eighth son. David's three older brothers are soldiers at the battle site, but the next four go unmentioned. So, we can assume that there are three sons who are 20 or older, and four sons younger than 20—then the youngest, David. While we don't know the exact age separation between the four sons, we could assume at least one year. David, then, is probably not older than 15. He's too young for the army, but still old enough to have developed fighting skills, such as a strong and accurate arm with the highly lethal sling, or slingshot.

David is insistent. "I'll go. I'll fight him!" Eventually, David wears down Saul's skepticism.

The king dismisses the shepherd boy with a sigh and a prayer. "Go, already! And may the Lord be with you!"

Shortly afterward, David strides onto the battlefield with only a few rocks, a slingshot and a vision. In the face of Goliath's taunts, David shouts out his statement of purpose: "I come to you in the name of the Lord of hosts, the God of the armies of Israel, whom you have defied."

Then comes his vision statement, announcing that he and God will bring into being a world in which "All the earth may know …

- That there is a God in Israel … [and]
- That the Lord does not save by sword and spear." (vs. 46-47)

David's vision is making God known to the world, linking Yahweh and Israel together, and demonstrating that God can rescue and deliver people without resorting to human weaponry.

There is a twofold scope to this vision. First, David's victory will not be a win just for David or just for Israel's army, but for the God previously regarded as simply another local deity. God's triumph will be of worldwide significance. Second, battle armaments will become less necessary in this envisioned world. David is not announcing a future of nonviolent pacifism, but he is radically challenging the paradigm that military victory is always secured by weaponry.

David brings into play what scholar Walter Brueggemann calls "an equalizer": David has God.

Leaders like David have a vision. Great leaders live by their commitment to a vision of a world that is bigger than personal success and for the betterment of humankind. Visions are frequently developed in times of patience, and often in our youthful years. If this is accomplished, then mature adults can bring leadership to their personal lives, their companies, their organizations, their clubs and even their families, by developing, clarifying and pursuing a vision.

The famous biblical proverb rightly states, "Where there is no vision, the people perish."

It's a powerful exercise to take the time to name some of the values you want to perpetuate by using your influence. You might prefer to use different, related terms to spark fresh reflections. What principles shape your life? What goals are important to you? What backs up your intentions to act? Is there anything you'd fight for, even against frightening odds, because it's that important to you?

Author Jonathan Swift said, "Vision is the art of seeing what is invisible to others."

There is a future that may be calling you alone. Pursue it. David shows us that a bold vision, rooted in God's purposes, is worth fighting for. Naming that God-fueled dream is the first step toward making it happen.

Without your vision, your unique future may well perish.

4

David Challenges Goliath

David said to the Philistine, "You come to me with sword and spear and javelin; but I come to you in the name of the Lord of hosts, the God of the armies of Israel, whom you have defied."

Highlights from 1 Samuel 17:1-58

A LEADER'S VISION may be a personal one—something held and nurtured over time. The opportunity to lead an organization can, at first, appear to be the chance to fulfill that vision. However, truly great leaders have to distinguish between their own interests and the best future for an organization.

The question is not "What do I want to do?" Rather, the question is this: "What needs to be done?"

Management consultant and author Peter Drucker wrote about Harry Truman suddenly becoming president in 1945. Truman had a vision of what he wanted to do: resume implementing Roosevelt's New Deal initiatives, which had been temporarily halted by World War II. However, as Truman became aware of the full range of issues confronting the U.S. at that time, he soon realized that foreign affairs were of much higher priority. The aftermath of an international war was claiming his fullest attention. Clinging to his personal vision when it did not align with the nation's best interest would have been selfish and irresponsible. Truman quickly realized that he needed to trade in his personal vision for his presidency for a vision of what the nation needed most at that time.

In a similar way, we can easily imagine that young David, having long served in his father's pastures, has nurtured personal dreams for himself. When the Goliath standoff arrives, he sees the battlefield as an excellent place to begin establishing his purpose. His vision could have been ego-driven: "I am the God-chosen future king of Israel, and today I'll prove it to the world." Or he could have decided that what was best was to elevate Israel by means of its army: "I will slay Goliath and prove that Israel's army is the most fearsome army of all."

But David determines that what is best for the nation of Israel is not to lift up himself or the army, but almighty God. He envisions proving that Israel's greatness lies not in any person or army, but in the God who established a covenant with Israel.

Vision is most powerful when the inspired idea, the abilities of the leader and the needs of an organization or nation all come together. Many new leaders of organizations take their posts under a previously established company mission or vision. Most leaders will face times when priorities have to be shifted and the vision adjusted, just as Harry Truman did in 1945. This concept may be somewhat different for entrepreneurs starting a new company: by definition, they usually have the opportunity to imprint their vision on the very identity of the organization. Yet this process of discernment still is crucial. Leaders and entrepreneurs alike must ask: "What is my own vision, and what is best for this new company at this time?"

Families are organizations, too. In fact, the family unit is considered by many to be the most fundamental organization in the world. Instead of being hired or drafted, members join by birth or marriage. But how often do family members ask the deeper organizational questions? They might ask, "What is the purpose of this family? Why are we here? What does God want of us? How can we fulfill our purpose?"

Just like David, families today can expect to confront scores of giants. It's never too early for family members to ask questions, such as: "What values do we aim to prioritize in our life together, in order to help each other thrive and grow with integrity?" Asking these questions can lead to exciting conversations among family members.

Remember that giants will loom. Infertility can dash the first draft of parents' dreams and force some significant rewriting. Children born with special needs may require parents and other family members to revise their expectations. Traumas, crises and losses entail similar readjustment—and, often, with little warning.

One day, I was sharing coffee in a parishioner's den after a neighborhood Bible study. I heard the story of a new mother who was shocked to learn that her newborn had Down syndrome. Her story began: "When I heard I was pregnant, I felt as if we were preparing for a wonderful trip. It's as if we were headed on a dream tour of Italy. It would be bright and sunny. We dreamed of the beaches, we looked forward to the pasta and the wines—we even imagined our child's Italian wedding."

Then came the surprise of Down syndrome. "It was as if we got off our trans-Atlantic flight and our captain announced that we had just landed in a snowy country far to the north of sunny Italy. There we were peering through the plane's windows, asking ourselves, 'Wait! Where are we?! We thought we were headed to our dream vacation in Italy. It's sleeting out there!'"

This story had a happy ending, though, as the woman, her husband and their entire family adjusted to the new reality. Fortunately, they had a vision that was ultimately rooted in values and principles. This vision sustained them when giant issues took them by surprise. Their values included patience, humility, love, forgiveness, courage and compassion. Values such as those endure, even when mental, physical and emotional capacities shift or decline. A vision built on deep values will teach all of us how to approach a situation when there may be things we cannot do.

By the time I heard this story, the family had been living in their new land for many years. Their child had enriched their lives in unexpected ways. "This is such a beautiful new country!" the mother was able to say. "Its history, its citizens, its spirit has meant the world to us. Sometimes we look back and wonder: What would Italy have been like for us? But that's just a passing thought. This is where we are, and it's a beautiful place to be."

The vision question for that family is the same as it was for David. The question is not "What do I want to do?" Instead, the question is "What needs to be done?"

Today, ponder the particular—and maybe even unique—needs of your family and community, and how they are now shaping your vision. What characteristics of a better, more just world are important to you? Do your priorities need to be adjusted in light of what's happening now?

If you keep a journal, consider listing some of the values you hold dear. You could even write them in the margins of this book, or in the space below; add today's date and then revisit them periodically. They may very well change over time.

How could you share your values with someone in your family or organization? Others can help you maintain your purpose and focus your energy as accountability partners. Perhaps they may even join you in making your vision become a reality.

5

David Defeats Goliath

David prevailed over the Philistine with a sling and a stone, striking down the Philistine and killing him; there was no sword in David's hand.

Highlights from 1 Samuel 17:1-58

THE END OF David's face-off with Goliath comes quickly. David announces his vision: God will be the victor, and traditional weaponry will play no part. David selects a stone, puts in in his slingshot and begins to whirl it. He lets the stone fly with such force that it sinks into Goliath's forehead. Goliath falls, face first, into the ground. He is dead. The battle is over.

Malcolm Gladwell, in his book *David and Goliath*, quotes an Israeli ballistics expert when explaining that David's stone, flung by a skilled slinger from a distance of, say, 35 meters, could easily have shattered Goliath's skull; this stone could have then entered his brain, rendering him unconscious or dead in a matter of seconds. It likely would have had the stopping force of a bullet from a moderately sized modern handgun.

The scene between David and Goliath reminds me of a scene in *Raiders of the Lost Ark*, when Indiana Jones is confronted by a daunting swordsman in the Egyptian marketplace. The swordsman intends to strike fear in our hero with an elaborate display of stances, moves and gestures, each of which could easily maim or kill an opponent. Jones looks at him for a moment, then simply pulls out a pistol and shoots him. The confrontation is over.

Before the encounter between David and Goliath, those who heard David's initial declarations may have smirked at what appeared to be empty boasting. Most of those on the battlefield that day probably did not pay too much attention to David's words, so engrossed as they were in what they assumed would be their roles in a titanic clash. David's astonishing victory changed everything! We can imagine stunned looks of disbelief all around.

Yet despite this bewildering success, David claims no personal credit for conquering Goliath. He points consistently to the power of God. David serves as a spokesman for God and a mediator of God's determination.

In this chapter, we continue reflecting on the power of vision to guide our lives, our families and our work. We know that organizations like to follow David's ancient example and present a bold mission or vision statement. Such declarations aim to make explicit an organization's purpose in the marketplace and the principles by which it will operate. Some of us may have had negative experiences with mission and vision statements—and for good reason, in many cases. At worst, developing a mission statement can be a boring waste of time. At best, however, these statements can serve as the constitution of an organization—the bedrock vision to which a company's leaders can return for guidance.

Let's take a look at a few corporate examples. A company's mission or vision can be explicitly religious:

- Chick-fil-A: "To glorify God by ..."
- Hobby Lobby: "To honor the Lord by ..."
- Interstate Batteries: "To glorify God as we ..."

Other companies don't invoke God explicitly, but their vision and values may be consistent with biblical virtues. Note the spiritual intentions in these statements:

- Starbucks: "To inspire and nurture the human spirit."
- Facebook: "To give people the power to build community and bring people closer together."
- Coca-Cola: "To refresh the world in mind, body and spirit."

How do you respond to these phrases? Learning some of the history of these organizations—as well as their accomplishments and failures over the years—will shape your reflections. Often, these statements turn out to be describing the founder's own, distinctive understanding of "God" or "human spirit." Both Chick-fil-A and Hobby Lobby have been involved in front-page news stories in recent years about their corporate under-standing of values. Starbucks founder Howard Schultz also has made front-page news for a short-lived presidential run. If you pull out your smartphone and begin to look around the internet, you'll find many other similarly thought-provoking mission statements. This day's reading could be another great discussion-starter with friends.

If you look a little further afield, you will discover that a guiding vision doesn't need to be flashy or innovative; on the contrary, it often can sound quite mundane. A vision may be as simple as "Be the best _____ in the world." That type of simple vision routinely inspires athletes, airlines, telecom giants, sports teams and small businesses alike.

Families can make their purposes explicit, too. Stephen Covey's *The 7 Habits of Highly Effective Families* includes multiple examples of family mission statements. These statements are often longer than the company statements above, and they frequently include a broad range of spiritual, interpersonal and social values.

Among Covey's examples:

- "Our Family Mission: To love each other ... To help each other ... To believe in each other ... To worship together ... Forever."
- "Our Family Mission: Value honesty with ourselves and others. ... Maintain patience through understanding. Always resolve conflicts with each other ..."

My wife, Beverly, has worked for years as a professional leadership coach. Her work often includes helping clients envision their desired future and then coaching them in taking steps toward that future. As we raised our two young sons, we had the opportunity (as all parents do) to shape our children's values and future. We often brought that opportunity into play at mealtime.

When we had the typical task of introducing new foods, we'd often say something like, "You like to try new things. Mom and Dad like to try new things, too. Let's try this." And in would come the broccoli or the fish or the yogurt. From early on, we helped shape their vision of themselves by affirming their openness to new experiences.

When other firsts arrived—a first day at school, a first day at summer camp—it was easy to anchor them in our family's values. We assured them that "we Buxtons like to try new things." Of course, life involves lots and lots of new things: starting a new job, moving to a new town or visiting a new vacation spot, for example. All of these changes can be sources of either deep anxiety or eagerly anticipated adventure. Today, both of our sons have worked in start-up companies, traveled to countries we've never seen and have even grown to love raw oysters! They like to try new things.

Vision is a magnet. A powerful vision—and, even, the *process* of shaping a vision—attracts and then pulls us steadily toward a life bigger than ourselves. We can help shape a world that's more just, more humane, more connected, more eco-friendly, more patient or more inclusive.

David's vision was not a self-aggrandizing statement of vanity. His larger purpose—to make God known—was central to the success of his confrontation with Goliath.

An early futurologist in the business world was Joel Barker, author of *Paradigms: The Business of Discovering the Future*. In it, he wrote:

"*Vision without action is merely a dream.*

Action without vision just passes the time.

Vision with action can change the world."

How have you begun to articulate a purpose for your family or your work? You can review your responses to yesterday's reading and perhaps build on them. What are the virtues you most want to cultivate in your family and pass on to the next generation? What are the values and visions that pull you, like a magnet, into each day?

Perhaps a sentence or two has begun to emerge from your thinking. Jot down those words. Use the pages of this book for notes, and add dates so that you can revisit those notes later—and perhaps discover changes in your life.

What would happen if you brought a conversation about values to the dinner table or into a conversation with a family member you trust? Barker encourages us not to just leave our thoughts and vision in the margins or recorded in a journal. No, it's the courage to act—to initiate sharing a forming vision—that can truly bring change to the world.

As we discern and cultivate God's vision for our lives, we can give "glory to God, who is able to do far beyond all that we could ask or imagine by his power at work within us." (Ephesians 3:20 CEB)

Humility

6

David Basks in Success

Saul commanded his servants, "Speak to David in private and
say: 'See, the king is delighted with you, and all his servants
love you; now then, become the king's son-in-law.'"

So Saul's servants reported these words to David in private. And
David said, "Does it seem to you a little thing to become the king's
son-in-law, seeing that I am a poor man and of no repute?"

Highlights from 1 Samuel 18:1-30

SEVERAL YEARS HAVE passed since David's victory over Goliath, and David has gone on to achieve widespread fame, additional military victories, the loyalty of soldiers and the adulation of a nation. David is described as having "success in all his undertakings."

The suspicious King Saul has kept David on the royal staff, first as a musician but now also so that he can keep a watchful eye on this potential rival. The king's daughter, Michal—having seen so much of the handsome and successful young man around the court—predictably falls in love with David. She wants to marry him.

Saul likes the idea. He calculates that a marriage between David and Michal could work to his advantage. So the king's attendants encourage David to take this big step and marry the boss's daughter. Saul is pulling the strings behind the scenes, and the servants are buzzing around David, encouraging him to take this big step.

The former shepherd boy has made a seemingly effortless ride to the top.

As the story unfolds, we notice one figure who is conspicuously absent: God. We've been told that the Lord is "with" David in a unique way, but Saul and Samuel seem to be the only ones who acknowledge that. David never shows any such awareness. God is missing from his musings and his conversation.

It is always dicey to argue a point from silence, but we can see that the narrator is noticeably silent about David's relationship with God. Even when David is encouraged to marry Michal and has a clear opportunity to praise God for this turn of events, he refers only to himself. "Me? Who am I and who are my kinsfolk … that I should be son-in-law to the king?" David makes no mention of God being an active contributor to his triumphs.

David's response in verse 23, which is nearly identical to his response in verse 18, is ambiguous at best. "Me? I am a poor man and of no repute." These sentences can be heard as an expression of humility: some translations use synonyms such as "common" and "without social standing," which reflect his shepherding origins. David was not born of royal stock.

Other translations make his protest seem rather hollow. In these accounts, David calls himself "lightly esteemed," "little known," "of no great name" and "insignificant." This is almost a direct contradiction of what has been said just a few verses earlier. David knows full well that he has "had success in all his undertakings," and his response may have the ring of phony humility and thinly disguised arrogance.

Either way, David has nothing to say for God in this entire account. His focus is his own ego. God is nowhere to be found.

Leadership expert Ken Blanchard suggests that EGO is an acronym for "Edging God Out." When God does not occupy a central place in one's value system, secondary concerns—the Bible calls them "gods" or "idols"— easily step in. These "lesser gods" do not inherently motivate us to do what is right, but rather, to do only what is in that idol's self-interest. If success, winning and personal achievement occupy the No. 1 position, then matters of how we treat others—fairness, compassion, collaboration, respect and so on—become secondary at best.

Too often, we act in a manner similar to David. How do we think of our lives when success comes easily and God seems irrelevant? Do we break out in song? "I did it *myyyy waaay!*" The self-made man, the rugged individualist, the lone fighter who beats all the odds—these are attractive stereotypes in American culture.

Biblically, this danger is both recognized and rebuked. "Do not say to yourself, 'My power and the might of my own hand have gotten me this wealth.' But remember the Lord your God, for it is he who gives you power to get wealth. ... If you do forget the Lord your God and follow other gods to serve and worship them, I solemnly warn you today that you shall surely perish." (Deuteronomy 8:17-19)

It's worth pondering what successes you've had that you have attributed to your own efforts. Where or when have you left God out of the picture? Have you assumed that your current achievements are all your own doing? Or, you might flip the questions around: What decisions have you made that you regret? What role, if any, did God play in those?

Several authors have been credited with the saying "Humility is not thinking less of yourself. It's thinking of yourself less." Pride, in essence, whispers, "I'm No. 1. I'm worth thinking about *all* the time."

Humility grows when we allow God to be No. 1 and take ourselves out of the spotlight. Where pride elevates us above God, humility lets us be recipients of God's grace.

"All of you must clothe yourselves with humility in your doings with one another, for 'God opposes the proud but gives grace to the humble.' Humble yourselves therefore under the mighty hand of God, so that [God] may exalt you in due time." (1 Peter 5:5-6)

How can we nurture humility in ourselves? Paradoxically, humility is a virtue that can enlarge our hearts and expand our influence.

7

Everybody Loves David?

*Saul set David over the army. And all the people, even the
servants of Saul, approved. All Israel and Judah loved David;
for it was he who marched out and came in leading them.*

*David had more success than all the servants of
Saul, so that his fame became very great.*

Highlights from 1 Samuel 18:1-30

IN JEWISH, CHRISTIAN and Islamic theology, humility is valued
as the proper disposition of a person in relation to God. Yet even without
an explicit belief in God, humility is still an important quality in a leader.
Today, a growing body of secular research is recommending humility as
the proper disposition of any person.

Put another way, humility can be considered both "vertically" and
"horizontally."

Vertically, humility is a measure of one's response to the First Com-
mandment: to love the Lord with all your heart, soul, mind and strength.
In addition, humility is a measure of one's response to the Second Com-
mandment, which is to love your neighbor as yourself.

For most of the 20th century, writing about humility was relegated
to the realm of religion. Scientists who studied psychology and social
interactions regarded humility as a hard-to-measure moral quality that
would not stand up to peer-reviewed research methods. In 2001, business
researcher Jim Collins changed all of that with his landmark book, *Good
to Great: Why Some Companies Make the Leap ... and Others Don't.* After
years of studying companies that made remarkable gains, Collins admitted
that his research team was "shocked" to discover that a rarely studied quality—humility—was the telling factor among exceptional leaders. Collins

called humility the defining quality in level 5 leadership. On a 1-to-5 scale of leadership qualities, Collins ranked humility at the top.

Until Collins rewrote the rules and backed them up with data, the phrase "humble leader" seemed to be an oxymoron. Our culture has long celebrated people such as Lee Iacocca, Rudy Giuliani, Steve Jobs, Roger Ailes and Donald Trump as the epitome of effective leaders. But in studying companies that have been successful over a 15-year period, Collins discovered that the most effective leaders demonstrated what we've called "horizontal" humility.

Sean Martin, a professor at the University of Virginia Darden School of Business, agrees. "The humble colleague is more likely to cultivate trust, encourage an exchange of ideas, help others develop while being open to their own areas for development, show empathy and generosity and succeed at work that requires change or assessment," Martin attests. "Humility leads to genuine collaboration—the cornerstone of any high-functioning team."

Collins' book was like a starter's gun for humility research in universities and think tanks. Now, there is a growing recognition that humility is a character strength that aligns with the collaborative nature of organizational life today. In 2019, Hogan Assessments—which produces psychological evaluation tools for more than half of the Fortune 500 companies—began offering its clients a "humility scale."

The capacity to encourage partnership and interdependence relies on lowering our individual hunger for praise and recognition. Humility can help businesses move from hierarchical, top-down structures to flatter configurations that encourage communication across all levels. Humility also signals an openness to continual learning, flexibility and empathy, which are key requirements for productive teamwork.

As researchers work to define what constitutes humble behavior in organizations, they're clearly discovering more ways in which humility is an asset to effectiveness.

Who has been an inspiring leader in your experience? What sort of personality calls forth your best efforts and energy? Can you recall a time when a boss inspired you to rise to a higher level in your work? Remember, this list can include family members. Your answers are good clues to the type of leader you may want to become.

Collins illustrates humility by using a window and a mirror. Top-quality leaders, he says, use the window to credit successes and the mirror to determine failures. Leaders who exhibit the trait he calls "deep personal empathy" do "routinely credit others, external factors and good luck for their company's success." They look out the window, seeing others as the source of their achievements. But when results are poor, they use the metaphorical mirror. They examine themselves.

The self-serving, less-humble leader does the opposite. Seeking to assign credit and blame, such a leader looks in the mirror to discover the source of accomplishment (self). The same leader looks out the window to find the source of failure (other people). A person like this makes excuses, shifts responsibility and complains about others.

Have you seen the "mirror and window" image at work? There are good assessment tools that can help you understand humility at work in your life. A 360-degree assessment, for example, is a carefully designed questionnaire through which you ask for personal feedback from people who surround you on a regular basis. The assessment is designed so that most individuals who participate aren't easily identifiable by you. For more information, talk with your HR department or a trained psychologist.

We can also get feedback from a trusted friend over coffee. Be careful about the questions you ask, lest you unleash a wave of trivial or hurtful comments. But a tactful truth-teller, a wise mentor or an honest and gentle co-worker can be a major asset.

So, what about David? What might he have heard over a cup of coffee? What can we say about his humility level? The short answer is "not much." We don't know. As the youngest of eight, David certainly knew a lot about cooperating with others and he had lots of experience with not getting his way. He had become resilient through listening and learning from others.

But, as a military officer, David had to use a more autocratic leadership style. He couldn't be distracted by focusing on the feelings and sentiments of the men under his command; he was their functional superior. Did everybody love David? We'll learn later on that the answer is obvious: of course not.

At the same time, every military officer has to earn the loyalty and devotion of his or her troops. This only happens through the ability to steer clear of an attitude of superiority and arrogance. Humility requires even the most autocratic leader to show compassion, care and empathy. David had to possess and practice this virtue, as a leader.

How are you showing humility in your interactions with your family or your co-workers? How are you fulfilling the command to "love your neighbor as yourself" at your kitchen table? Or the company cafeteria? Or the soccer field?

As advised by the wise Albert Einstein, "Try not to become a person of success, but rather a person of value."

Integrity

8

David Faces a Test

Saul took 3,000 chosen men out of all Israel and went to look for David and his men in the direction of the Rocks of the Wild Goats. He came to the sheepfolds beside the road, where there was a cave; and Saul went in to relieve himself.

Now David and his men were sitting in the innermost parts of the cave. The men of David said to him, "Here is the day of which the Lord said to you, 'I will give your enemy into your hand, and you shall do to him as it seems good to you.'"

Highlights from 1 Samuel 24:1-22

SAUL'S PARANOIA AND hostility toward David, the rising star of the royal court, continues to grow. Chapters 1 Samuel 18 through 24 describe Saul moving David out of the court to become the commander of 1,000 men. Saul is increasingly convinced that David is out to kill him, so Saul and his soldiers begin chasing David throughout the hilliest, rockiest areas of Israel. If you follow David's flight, he zigzags across great swaths of Israel, moving through jagged, mountainous terrain.

For first-time visitors of Israel, the country's extreme barrenness and rugged geography may come as a surprise. On my first visit, I remember thinking, "The No. 1 crop that Israel produces is rocks!" Everywhere I looked, the ground was pushing up boulders, mountains, crags, peaks and cliffs. Parts of Israel look like Mars. There are areas so rocky and undeveloped that the caves pock-marking the mountainside look like the windows of a housing project.

If you read through the chapters that describe David's running from town to town and hiding in caves, the text is almost comical. There are repeated episodes of rumor, pursuit, escape and frustration. It's like madcap farce, slowed to a snail's pace; it's amusing, except for the fact that Saul and David are playing a deadly game.

Saul follows the latest rumor and chases David into the wilderness of Engedi, which means "place of the spring goats." It's a small oasis west of the Dead Sea, high in the craggy mountains and not far from the Qumran Caves. Of all the territory that these two men and their armies have been crisscrossing, it is when Saul suddenly needs to go to the bathroom that he has the incredible misfortune of walking into the exact cave in which David and his men are hiding. Here there is both humor and pathos, absurdity and sadness. Israel's powerful king finally shares the same space as his enemy, but it's unintentional and without awareness. As Saul hikes up his robe to relieve himself, he exposes his most private parts before his rival.

David's men urge him to take advantage of his position and strike Saul while he is vulnerable. David recoils from the suggestion, but then moves quickly toward Saul. While Saul is squatting, David stealthily cuts off a portion of the hem of his robe. David then feels guilty about doing even that—taking advantage of Saul in such a vulnerable way.

Saul finishes his business and leaves the cave, and David soon follows him. David hollers Saul's name, greets him humbly from a distance, and begins a shouted conversation about what just happened.

It's only when David tells the story and holds up a piece of Saul's robe that the king realizes his humiliating vulnerability in the cave. David challenges Saul to rethink his irrational hatred. David explains why he spared Saul's life.

David's long speech (verses 8-15) has four points:

1. Killing Saul would simply be wrong. "The Lord forbid that I should do this thing … I will not raise my hand against my lord." (v. 10b; also v. 6) David will do what is right, in spite of his feelings. He has integrity. He keeps faith with his principles in the face of what is advantageous.

2. Sparing Saul shows courage. David stood up against his fellow soldiers, who advised him to take advantage of Saul's exposure. "Some urged me to kill you, but I spared you." (v. 10; also v. 7) David can stand strong against harmful advice.

3. David's mercy is proof that he is not a wicked man. The ancient proverb (v. 13) states, "Out of the wicked comes forth wickedness." If David were, in fact, evil, Saul would be dead. But since Saul is alive, David did no evil and is therefore not an evil man. Saul is mistaken about him.

4.   David is ready to lay the matter humbly before God. He is eager
     to convince Saul that he is in the right and Saul in the wrong, but
     he's also humble enough to submit the matter to God's verdict.
     "May the Lord therefore be judge and give sentence between me
     and you." (v. 15; also v. 12)

David winces at the idea of winning at all costs. He stands by the choice
he made in the cave. He chooses integrity.

Centuries later another military leader, Dwight Eisenhower, proclaimed
the same virtue to be essential. "The supreme quality for leadership is,
unquestionably, integrity. Without it, no real success is possible."

Integrity is more important to David than "winning ugly." Tennis
coach Brad Gilbert popularized that phrase in his book of the same title.
He meant that sometimes, an athlete will need to win by just "grinding it
out"; the victory doesn't have to be graceful or pretty. David's notion of
"winning ugly" is different. He refuses to win at any cost. He will not betray
his conscience and his values by stooping low, just to win.

Winning ugly has dishonorable examples across sports. It's the order in
The Karate Kid to attack the wounded Daniel with a leg sweep; it's hitting
below the belt in boxing; it's sucker-punching wrestler John Cena when
the referee's back is turned; it's moving the golf ball out of a difficult lie; it's
tripping a player on the basketball court. Perhaps it is withholding information that one is duty-bound to share.

David's integrity invites us to consider how we've treated our opponents
in conflicts past or present. Have you ever felt pressured to act against your
better judgment? Have you done so and "won ugly"? How do you feel
about that now?

Conversely, have you ever passed up a chance to win for the sake of
your conscience? Maybe you missed getting something you wanted by
refusing to pay the moral price. What faith values would you use to justify
your (or David's) action?

The Bible promises vindication to everyone who endures suffering and
disappointment in the short run for standing strong in God's purpose.

• "You have upheld me because of my integrity, and set me in your
  presence forever." (Psalm 41:12)

- "I consider that the sufferings of this present time are not worth comparing with the glory about to be revealed to us." (Romans 8:18)

- "May you be … made strong with all the strength that comes from his glorious power, and may you be prepared to endure everything with patience, while joyfully giving thanks to the Father, who has enabled you to share in the inheritance of the saints in the light." (Colossians 1:11-12)

In that cave long ago, David clearly had the opportunity to eliminate Saul and claim the throne of Israel. But the cost to his integrity was too great. In his actions and words, David demonstrated a supreme quality for leadership: integrity.

9

A Righteous Man

When David had finished speaking these words to Saul, Saul said—
"You are more righteous than I; for you have repaid me good, whereas I have
repaid you evil. Today you have explained how you have dealt well with
me, in that you did not kill me when the Lord put me into your hands. For
who has ever found an enemy, and sent the enemy safely away? So may
the Lord reward you with good for what you have done to me this day."

Highlights from 1 Samuel 24:1-22

IN SHOWING MERCY to King Saul at a vulnerable moment, David renounces the idea of winning "by any means necessary." He will not claim that the end justifies the means. He can never know what the end will be, or if that will ever be "the end." The means are all that he can control. David chooses an uncertain future with his integrity intact over a sure victory that would cost him his soul.

We remember that in his brief speech to Saul, David makes four points. In those arguments he points to four core values (in this book, we will also call them virtues):

1. **Morality.** "Thou shalt not kill" is a basic tenet of almost every moral code. While nuances and qualifications exist, there is universal agreement that murdering an unarmed person by surprise is simply wrong. "Moral authority comes from following universal and timeless principles like honesty, integrity, treating people with respect." (Covey) If moral authority is compromised, all other assumptions of fairness and trust are undermined, and the organization (be it a nation, a church, a company or a family) is in trouble. David knew that killing Saul would be wrong. Moral strength is essential for a leader.

2. **Courage.** Leadership requires courage. A leader cannot simply "agree with the last person he talks to," or the organization will be rife with suspicion. If the one who is trusted to take others into new and strange territory wilts under opposition, failure is assured. The leader must be able to resist peer pressure and stay dedicated to the vision. David did this.

3. **Mercy.** Mercy lets go of the past in service of the future. Showing mercy demonstrates that the future is more important than the past. Retribution is a counterproductive and often destructive choice for leaders. Even though Saul seeks to kill David, David does not retaliate. David's mercy requires inner strength.

4. **Humility.** Great leaders avoid endless explaining and justifying. With both humility and respect, they can lay down their work for judgment before God and others. Leaders don't have to be right at all costs; they can let their actions speak for themselves and receive whatever judgment or approval may come. David invites God to be the judge.

Morality, courage, mercy and humility. These four virtues undergird David's integrity as he speaks to Saul (vs. 8-15). Saul responds graciously. "So may the Lord reward you with good for what you have done to me this day. Now I know that you shall surely be king." David's integrity has saved the day and convinced the king.

We have to be honest, though. Few movie directors would end a film with this scene. We have to admit that these qualities are not universally applauded in our culture.

Football coach Vince Lombardi was frequently quoted as saying, "Winning isn't everything; it's the only thing." The quote originated with another coach, but Lombardi repeated it enough to have it attributed to him. There's great pressure on a leader to be tough enough to "do what needs to be done." When results are on the line, organizations often wonder if the boss can "close the deal" or "pull the trigger." Acts of conscience can be seen as "going soft." Employees have to be team players.

Leaders, in turn, may justify dubious actions by saying something such as, "Well, I'm doing it just this one time." Personal integrity may seem like a luxury when other people's incomes and futures are riding on a decision.

We convince ourselves that the end justifies the means; the goal is more important than how we get there.

Temptation never comes dressed in a devil's red suit with a pitchfork. It dresses respectably and speaks rationally. That's why it can be so persuasive. Have there been times when you've felt the power of temptation's attraction? How did you handle it? Did you recognize the temptation before or after your action?

These are the very situations we pray for when we pray the Lord's Prayer: "Lead us not into temptation, but deliver us from evil." Temptation always comes with compelling reasons and persuasive justifications. But the price is high. "What good would it be for someone to gain the whole world, yet forfeit their soul?" (Matthew 16:26)

Leaders who choose integrity over success are making a courageous choice. These leaders look beyond short-term implications and onward, to the long-term effect. You show who you are by what you do. Has acting with integrity ever cost you deeply? On the contrary, has it ever rewarded you deeply?

Alan Simpson, a former U. S. senator from Wyoming, is widely admired for his strength of character. His words are worth contemplating today:

"If you have integrity, nothing else matters.

If you don't have integrity, nothing else matters."

David—in his encounter with Saul in the cave, at least—shows us a leader unafraid to embrace the virtue of integrity. He will not always remember that, or always resist the power of temptation. But in this instance, standing before Saul, he lives and speaks the truth. Nothing else matters.

Openness

10

Abigail Disrupts David's Plan

When Abigail saw David, she hurried and alighted from the donkey, and fell before David on her face, bowing to the ground and saying: "My lord, do not take seriously this ill-natured fellow, Nabal; for as his name is, so is he; Nabal is his name, and folly is with him .... Now then, my lord, as the Lord lives, and as you yourself live, since the Lord has restrained you from bloodguilt and from taking vengeance with your own hand, now let your enemies and those who seek to do evil to my lord be like Nabal."

Highlights from 1 Samuel 25:2-42

DAVID'S COMPLEXITY IS beginning to emerge. He's a man of integrity and humility, yet he's also got a prickly temper. His propensity for violence continues to lurk just below the surface. The full account of David's encounter with Abigail makes for an absorbing and amusing reading. You will recall that 1 Samuel 18 marks the beginning of a long section detailing Saul's paranoid pursuit of David, and for years, David zigzagged through the mountains and deserts of Israel and Judah. This story takes place during that time.

While David and his soldiers were in the wilderness of Paran, southwest of the Dead Sea, they encountered the servants of a man named Nabal. The servants were out shearing their master's sheep. David's soldiers watched over the shearers for a time, protecting them from roving bandits and wild animals. After the shearers returned to Nabal's household, David sent a delegation of soldiers to Nabal on a feast day. He asked Nabal to provide a banquet for his men, in order to show his appreciation for their protection and to celebrate the festival.

Nabal regards David's request as a shakedown. (Verse 13 reveals that David has 600 men under his command; this is, therefore, no small request, and Nabal may be right.) Nabal senses the intimidation behind

David's appeal, and he refuses to hand over that much food to a man he doesn't even know. When the soldiers bring the message back to David, he is insulted and furious. "Strap on your swords," he barks to his men. David and 400 of his soldiers set off to Nabal's house to slaughter the entire household. This is the worst of David's hot temper.

A sympathetic soldier tips off Nabal's wife, Abigail, about the upcoming slaughter. Abigail springs into action. Without telling her husband, she prepares a huge feast of food and sends out her servants and their loaded donkeys. She intercepts David and pleads her case directly to him.

In essence, Abigail says that her husband is an idiot. (In Hebrew, "Nabal" actually means "fool," or "idiot." Abigail says that he definitely lives up to his name.) Abigail continues: "Just ignore him. I want to apologize and will gladly feed your soldiers, O king. I also want to save you from incurring the guilt and condemnation that would be yours if you slaughtered my household. You truly have God's favor as a warrior and as a future king. Don't do this. Have a clean heart as you go forward. The Lord has a great future in store for you."

David listens, praises God and blesses Abigail for her intervention. He takes to heart her approach to the conflict, and he changes his mind. David lets go of his anger, accepts her gift and sends her home in peace.

The story of this encounter is so moving that great artists and writers have recreated the meeting, down through the centuries, as an illustration of peacemaking. In the 17th century, Peter Paul Rubens painted large canvases of the scene a number of times, including one that served as the model for a tapestry of the meeting. In more recent years the scene continues to be shared, even as an internet meme labeled "Abigail the Peacemaker."

Tomorrow we'll ponder David's openness to having his plans challenged by an "outsider." Today, let's look at how David considers an alternative approach to resolving conflict. (I am indebted to the work of Patricia Heim, Tammy Hughes and Susan Murphy *et al.* for material in this section.)

Social science research has consistently highlighted differences in the way that men and women communicate and solve disagreements. David demonstrates what has been called a "male approach" to managing conflict.

As leaders, men often establish a culture that holds certain assumptions about power, such as:

- Power is the ability to push your agenda through to your desired outcome.
- There is only one boss, and the boss is not to be challenged.
- Win-lose strategies are acceptable.
- Be aggressive. If resisted, be ready to counter-punch and escalate.
- If you have power, use it. Don't "go soft" or "chicken out." Be decisive.

By contrast, there is a so-called "female approach" in which women often operate from different assumptions, such as:

- Power is the ability to negotiate a shared solution that is better than any one person can formulate.
- Decisions can be discussed.
- Seek win-win strategies whenever possible.
- Look for ways to de-escalate conflict.
- It can be wise to change your mind, to adjust your course of action and to slow down the process.

How do you respond to the statements above? We know that they do not describe *all* men or *all* women, of course. In fact, assumptions about gender are rapidly evolving. Perhaps you reject Heim's references to "male" and "female" approaches to conflict. Removing gender from the description, these approaches have also been described as "insisting power" and "negotiating power."

Where have you experienced these different approaches to power? In your home? At the office? Within your congregation? Among friends?

Scriptures are familiar with both approaches to conflict management. "Insisting power" is used most frequently, since the Bible is set in a patriarchal time of monarchies and military rulers. But the message of Jesus and his followers is generally biased toward the latter, the less "insistent" style of using power.

Think about the approaches described by these leaders:

- Jesus: "You know that those who are regarded as rulers of the Gentiles lord it over them, and their high officials exercise authority over them. Not so with you." (Mark 10:42f.)
- Paul: "I do not mean to imply that we lord it over your faith; rather, we are workers with you for your joy, because you stand firm in the faith." (2 Corinthians 1:24)
- Peter: "[Leadership is ...] not bossily telling others what to do, but tenderly showing them the way." (1 Peter 5:3 from *The Message* paraphrase)

There are many different ways of approaching conflict. Even within congregations, you may be thinking of times when a rabbi or pastor used "insisting power" as readily as "negotiating power." No one way fits every situation. As organizational consultant Simon Sinek stated, "One of the best paradoxes of leadership is a leader's need to be both stubborn and open-minded."

Are there times when one form of conflict approach should predominate? What are some of these times? Might you be called to use one of these approaches in your life this week?

Whatever the setting, we're wise to open our hearts and listen carefully to different styles, just as David did. Regardless of which tactic may be needed at a given time, the very act of listening and considering may itself be the surest path to peace.

David Heeds Abigail's Advice

David said to Abigail, "Blessed be the Lord, the God of Israel, who sent you to meet me today! Blessed be your good sense, and blessed be you, who have kept me today from bloodguilt and from avenging myself by my own hand!"

Highlights from 1 Samuel 25:2-22

KING DAVID ACTUALLY listens to a woman. What's more, he changes his mind and agrees with her! What is going on here? Given gender assumptions in the ancient world, David's men must have been baffled.

Today, gender differences continue to play a significant role in the life of every organization. Depending on your age, you may recall women's liberation movements, the "Year of the Woman," numerous women's marches and the #MeToo movement. You'll spark a spirited discussion with friends if you ask them to simply reflect on these ever-evolving concepts. It's well worth the effort, because multiple forms of discrimination still hinge on concepts of gender.

Centuries after David, the apostle Paul proclaimed, "There is neither Jew nor Greek; there is neither slave nor free; nor is there male and female, for you are all one in Christ Jesus." (Galatians 3:28) The ministry of Jesus and the witness of the early church consistently commands us to break down gender barriers and welcome all sources of wisdom and leadership.

Most of us are familiar with the way women were marginalized in Jesus' time. We know that the Gospels are full of stories of women who were considered scandalous, untouchable and unclean. Women were often avoided or dismissed. When the disciples heard the first accounts of Jesus' resurrection from women, they initially dismissed the women's account altogether. They regarded this news as foolishness, silly talk, even "twaddle."

Not only was the news radical; the women, simply by being women, were considered *ipso facto* unreliable messengers.

David's era was roughly a thousand years prior to Jesus. Abigail represented for David a doubtful, suspicious source of wisdom. David's openness to Abigail is radical!

Today, congregations are increasingly recognizing that wisdom comes from people young or old, with more or less experience, and with or without seniority. Wisdom may come from people of different spoken languages, gender identities, colors and faiths. This is a natural extension of what we all are learning in our schools, our places of work, our neighborhoods—and even within our own families.

Perhaps you have a friendship with someone whom you first dismissed as being "different." How did you come to value this person? How did you become open to the value of what he or she had to offer you? What good advice or example have you received from someone who was "different"? Diversity is a valuable gift that God gives to us, and openness is the appropriate response.

Churches have also been emphasizing the importance of hospitality in recent years. Many of us have come to understand that despite our believing we're part of a welcoming congregation, visitors and guests may not experience it that way. We've had to learn more intentional ways of showing hospitality to others. How has your congregation (if you participate in one) or organization opened you to practice deeper hospitality?

Consider "openness" from an even broader perspective. Everything you have ever learned came from a position of openness. There were times when you did not know something, so you listened or watched. You considered the importance of what you were observing. You may have fought off the impulse to argue or leave. Slowly, you began to welcome this new insight or skill. You made room in your mind or heart to accommodate new realities.

Consider your own journey in faith. At some point you welcomed a new word or a fresh voice that you hadn't previously encountered. You learned to be hospitable to biblical truths taught by others. Openness is the spiritual heart of our orientation to life itself. Are we open to the adventure that each new day brings? Or are we wary and anxious about the unknown? Some of us feel that to live means to *survive*—and we can only do that by being cautious, holding to what's proven to be true and staying skeptical of what is new. Others feel that to live means to *thrive*, and that's done by taking risks, holding lightly to the status quo and welcoming the new.

One year, while I was a young adult, I worked as a counselor at a summer camp. The camp had a tradition of welcoming a small number of counselors from other countries each summer. That year there were three out-of-country counselors, hailing from Lebanon, Spain and the Ivory Coast. I became friends with the counselor from the Ivory Coast, in particular, who was an ebullient young man named Kouassi. He taught me—and on a daily basis, we carried out—one of the traditions from his country, Cote d'Ivoire. Each morning, he would greet me by saying my name and asking me a question posed by the French word for "Yes." Each day, he would smile and say, "Larry, oui?"

I would say, "Oui. Kouassi, oui?"

And, he'd reply "Oui."

In doing this, he was asking me if I would say "Yes" to the day ahead. Was I open to the blessings and good things in store for me that day? Was I beginning my day ready to receive whatever new events the day would bring? I'd say "Oui," then ask him the same. In doing so, we were declaring our openness to whatever the day would bring, sustained by a shared belief in a kind and loving God.

All learning and growth is rooted in openness. Similarly, Charles Kettering, the co-founder of the Memorial Sloan Kettering Cancer Center, said, "Where there is an open mind, there will always be a frontier." It's up to us whether we find frontiers exciting or frightening.

I believe that hospitality is God's bias toward choosing the risk of welcoming what's new. It's not simply swallowing whatever new fad comes along, but rather it is a spiritual orientation toward the creation and its creator, the one who says, "Behold! I make all things new."

Perhaps, like me, you're still learning to welcome the spiritual wisdom and insights that come from people who don't necessarily look, sound or think like you. By doing so, you're remembering that "God shows no partiality" (Romans 2:11; cf. Acts 10:34) and that God has made us sisters and brothers with folks from all corners of the earth.

David models for us this unexpected openness. We become more like God by receiving the surprising encounters and conversations of daily life with hospitality and openness.

Tenderness

David Mourns Saul and Jonathan

Then David sang this funeral song for Saul and his son Jonathan: "Oh, no, Israel! Your prince lies dead on your heights. Look how the mighty warriors have fallen!"

Highlights from 2 Samuel 1:1-27

DAVID'S BOYHOOD IS over. Gone are the days of sheep and sling-shots. He's a young man now, probably in his mid- to late 20s, married and an officer in Israel's army. He'd found a mentor in Saul and a soulmate in Saul's son, Jonathan. Saul was a complex figure in David's development, to be sure, but he was a formative one, too. War with the Philistines has erupted again, and at a significant battle on Mt. Gilboa, both Saul and Jonathan are killed. The two most important men in David's life now lie dead.

When this news comes back to David, he doesn't put on a mask of macho stoicism. No, David weeps and grieves openly for the deaths of these two valiant men. Tenderness is on full display.

Let's listen in:

"Oh, no, Israel!" Most of us are familiar with comparing various English translations of the Bible to try to understand the power of the original Hebrew in today's terms. For this particular passage, I like the raw shock and grief of David's words that come to us in the Common English Bible: "Oh, no, Israel! Your prince lies dead …! Look how the mighty warriors have fallen." David laments the loss his nation has suffered. Saul and Jonathan were powerful protectors of their people, and their absence is so terrifying that we hear David calling out, "Don't talk about it … don't bring news of it."

Israel is vulnerable. David is distraught.

David's lament over Saul and Jonathan seems to move to a deeper level, as he grieves for more than their military prowess. He laments over the loss of the character they embodied. They were loved and cherished. David praises their loyalty, their courage and their generosity: "They were never separated. They were ... stronger than lions! Daughters of Israel, Saul dressed you in crimson with jewels." We hear David say that Israel has lost brave, devoted and generous leaders.

Finally, David tears open his own heart: "I grieve for you, my brother Jonathan! You were so dear to me." We can pretty much hear David sobbing at this point. The loss isn't just for his nation; David's own profound grief pours forth. His heart is broken. The pain has cut deep, and he weeps. Walter Brueggemann calls this lament David's "long, slow singing—an act of courage."

David is a sobbing king, a crying warrior. How jarring is this? Early in our lives, most of us hear a parent or teacher say, "Stop crying!" Many men live with the mistaken impression that manhood itself—much less leadership—requires stoicism. Men are taught that tears are weak, and that they have to "man up" and stay focused on business. Even pastors, male and female alike, may feel expected to be "above it all"—to exemplify their devotion to higher realities by putting emotion aside and leading with impassiveness. What messages have you received since childhood about crying or showing deep emotion in public?

The 20th century American poet Vachel Lindsay challenged the emotionless ideal for men:

> "Only boys keep their cheeks dry.
>
> Only boys are afraid to cry.
>
> Men thank God for tears."

Lindsay invites men to see wet cheeks as a sign of maturity. Giving oneself permission to fully experience loss and grief is a sign of strength. A 13th century Italian poet, Dante Aligheri, said something similar:

> "I wept not,
>
> so to stone I grew."

Our very humanity is at stake here. Tenderness is not weakness. David's mourning comes from a mature and fully human heart.

In the professional world, crying is often seen as the very definition of *un*professional, despite the fact that tears can be as involuntary as a case of hiccups. In *Hardball for Women: Winning at The Game of Business*, author Pat Heim encourages women to develop strategies for coping with tears that may come at an unwanted time. For example, someone may simply say, "I care a great deal about this, and I might cry when we talk about it. Please don't let that distract you from what I want to say."

When has deep emotion spilled out of you at an unexpected time? How did you handle it? In what ways might these unexpected emotions have been beneficial for you?

Tears at the top—deep emotion from one's leader—can be a powerful gift. When President Barack Obama spoke about the December 2012 Sandy Hook Elementary School shooting, he did so with deep feeling and a wounded heart. While giving remarks around that time, he was shown biting his lip, wiping his eyes, pausing to steady himself, letting his voice catch and shedding tears.

"Showing empathy and vulnerability makes a leader seem stronger, not weaker," says John Gerzema, CEO of the global BAV Consulting. In the famously brief verse, "Jesus wept" (John 11:35), it is affirmed that the divine son of God wasn't impervious to human suffering. On the contrary, he was intimately immersed in it. No one thought Jesus to be less of a savior because of his wet cheeks. How does pondering this verse affect your faith?

David's faith was big enough to embrace this paradox that's worthy of pondering—or worthy of discussion, if you're with a group. Consider the following:

> *To share your weakness is to make yourself vulnerable.*
>
> *To make yourself vulnerable is to show your strength.*

In his tears, David shows the cardinal virtue of tenderness.

13

David Grows From Grief

David took hold of his clothes and tore them; and all the men who were with him did the same. They mourned and wept, and fasted until evening for Saul and for his son Jonathan, and for the army of the Lord and for the house of Israel, because they had fallen by the sword.

Highlights from 2 Samuel 1:1-27

ACCORDING TO SOME Bibles in English translation, David is "distressed" about Jonathan's death—but that is a wimpy interpretation. Synonyms for "distressed" include "worried," "anxious," "upset" and "concerned," but David is in full-blown grief. Better translations describe David as heartbroken, crushed, grieving, crying and weeping.

David's grief invites us to reconsider the value in the maxim often attributed to Theodore Roosevelt, among others: "People don't care how much you know until they know how much you care." No matter how skilled, intelligent, ambitious or bold any leader may be, followers will be in short supply if they don't feel you care about them.

Grief is a gift that opens our hearts to valuing other people. It often forces us to slow down or stop, to recall the blessings we knew through another person, and to honor the simple details that made up our interactions with them. Insensitive leaders—those who don't take the time to listen and value others—will most likely see an ongoing exodus from their ranks. Parents who are too busy to savor the miracle of children and family will find themselves sad and alone in years to come. We can easily remember Harry Chapin's song-parable "Cat's in the Cradle," and the sad undercurrent of realizing that the too-busy father is soon brushed aside by his too-busy son.

Grief will impact every single leader, for the simple reason that every leader is a human being. Following the terrorist attacks on Sept. 11, 2001, Queen Elizabeth said, "Grief is the price we pay for love." No life can remain untainted by sorrow and heartache, the persistent companions of death. But we can grow by becoming aware of the blessings of grief. Grief can undergird our work of guiding and influencing others.

Grief forces us to step back and reassess the appearance of normalcy in daily life. Our days with each other come and go with astonishing velocity. Virtues that speed by unnoticed will come into focus when grief slows things down.

Look again at David's lament. David names the qualities that, all jumbled together, made Saul and Jonathan admirable men: their devotion to their country, their loyalty to each other, their courage and prowess in battle. Those with whom David had mixed feelings and dealings at the time—especially Saul—can still be honored, from a higher perspective, as mighty leaders.

David eulogizes Saul as one who "dressed [Israel] in crimson with jewels; he decorated your clothes with gold jewelry." This is odd praise, in that the tribes under Saul's leadership always remained rather poor. They never had gold and jewels. But Saul gave the tribes a sense of dignity and respect among other peoples, leading them from a scattered tribal confederation to a genuine nation-state. Grief enables David to judge Saul more compassionately.

David's lament makes an interesting rhetorical move. In speaking of Saul, David elevates Saul's legacy over his feelings for him. David deliberately sets aside his personal sentiment. There was clearly little love lost between the two men, but David can honestly praise Saul's legacy and recognize what he accomplished as Israel's king.

When speaking of Jonathan, David takes the opposite approach. While Jonathan was no slouch as a military figure, David barely touches on his abilities as a warrior; instead, he focuses his grief on Jonathan's heart—on his deep love for David and David's love for him. Our faith teaches us that every soul in the world has unique, sacred value. This means that every person, be he enemy or friend, can be honored and eulogized with integrity. Grief can give us the ability to dignify both those we love and those with whom we differ.

Grief can refine our hearts. We learn to stop sweating the small stuff and see the bigger picture. Petty differences shrink as more important values and memories rise to the surface. This is an opportunity to become more patient. When life ends suddenly, we develop a greater appreciation for its fragility and the importance of being attentive to what makes life so precious.

Thornton Wilder's play *Our Town* consistently ranks high on lists of most important American plays and most frequently performed American plays. It won the 1938 Pulitzer Prize for drama. *Our Town* tells the story of fictional Grover's Corners in the earliest years of the 20th century. The narrative comes through the words of the town's inhabitants. In one of its most poignant scenes, a deceased child named Emily is granted her wish to revisit just one day of earthly life.

Emily watches an ordinary day unfold before her eyes, and she is simply overcome with emotion. She says:

> "Let's really look at one another! ... It goes so fast. We don't have time to look at one another. I didn't realize. So, all that was going on and we never noticed ... Wait! One more look. Good-bye, Good-bye world. Good-bye, Grover's Corners ... Mama and Papa. Good-bye to clocks ticking ... and Mama's sunflowers. And food and coffee. And new ironed dresses and hot baths ... and sleeping and waking up. Oh, earth, you are too wonderful for anybody to realize you. Do any human beings ever realize life while they live it—every, every minute?"

It's often been said that the heart of spiritual life is simply paying attention. Grief can move us toward renewing a commitment to a spiritual life, because grief demands that we pause and reflect on what's truly important. Self-reflection and new awareness are common gifts of grief.

In the process, grief can make us more compassionate. We can cultivate an inner tenderness that can help us connect to others in more personal ways. Does a person's showing vulnerability help you feel closer or more empathic toward that person than you did before?

How has grief impacted your life for the better? Has that experience encouraged you to nurture your tender side? Or has it had the opposite effect?

Of course, tenderness of the heart doesn't *require* the searing experience of grief; no, the benefits of heartache and anguish can come in other ways, too. Leadership resources such as Kouzes and Posner's *Encouraging the Heart* and Richard Phillips' *The Heart of an Executive* remind us that the simple act of developing the best qualities of our humanity can improve relationships.

Yet the blessings of grief, in particular, can deepen an essential style of leadership that values consideration, tenderness, empathy and compassion.

Forgiveness

14

David's Rivals Ask for Forgiveness

Then all the tribes of Israel came to David at Hebron, and said, "Look, we are your bone and flesh. For some time, while Saul was king over us, it was you who led out Israel and brought it in. The Lord said to you: 'It is you who shall be shepherd of my people Israel, you who shall be ruler over Israel.'"

So, all the elders of Israel came to the king at Hebron; and King David made a covenant with them at Hebron before the Lord, and they anointed David king over Israel.

Highlights from 2 Samuel 5:1-5

AFTER KING SAUL'S death, the northern tribes joined together and installed Saul's son, Ishbaal, as their king. David was acknowledged as king only in the southern region of Judah. Over time, however, Ishbaal's forces grew weaker and Ishbaal was assassinated by soldiers seeking David's favor. Now, the leaders of the 10 tribes come together to ask their former enemy for help.

The exact chronology is much disputed, but the time is most likely around 1077 BCE. The leaders of the northern tribes of Israel now come to David, who is about 30 years old. They are frightened. They come to surrender and to plead for mercy. They have battled him for years, but now they seek his benevolent rule. They have killed his soldiers; now they come to him in hopes for peace.

These leaders appeal to David, and they say three things. Their triad of pleading is based on three components:

- **Relationship.** "We are your very own flesh and bone," they tell David, reminding him of their kinship and shared ancestry. They are all descendants of the original 12 tribes from long ago. They hope that their appeal to the deep bonds of blood connection might discourage vengeance.

- **Accomplishment**. "When Saul ruled over us, you were the one who led Israel out to war and back." The tribes have benefitted from David's triumphs and accomplishments, and they acknowledge his achievements. Saul was the designated ruler, true, but they recognize David as the "muscle" behind the throne.
- **Promise**. "The Lord told you, 'You will shepherd my people, and you will be Israel's leader.'" The tribes affirm God's promise to David concerning his divine destiny. In doing this, they implicitly confess faith in David's God and choose to follow David's divinely ordained rule.

The Bible tells us the words of the tribal elders, but not the words of David's response. His response is summed up in the narrator's words: "King David made a covenant with them." The writer may well feel that actions speak louder than words, but David's relative silence shouldn't lure us into thinking that his response was automatic.

Granting forgiveness is difficult work, and David was faced with a number of ways to respond. He could refuse; he could gloat; he could punish; he could demand extreme demonstrations of loyalty. David could make his victory especially hard for Israel to swallow, forever "reminding them who's boss."

Have you ever found yourself in a similar situation? Someone comes to you and, in essence, says, "You were right all along. I was wrong, and I want to be on your side again." There are an infinite number of ways this appeal may have come to you. Perhaps the person before you used words of apology; perhaps (as in David's encounter) no words of guilt or apology were uttered. Has this happened to you? How did you respond?

On the other hand, maybe you have been the one choosing words to say to someone else. You've wanted to undo something that was done or said. It takes courage to have such a conversation, and often, we choose to ignore the conflict. Too frequently, we "put it behind us" and "move on." But when a face-to-face conversation is needed, the virtue of courage is your ally. What was the reaction of the person you spoke to?

Many leaders need to learn how to lose graciously. Many more of us need to learn how to win graciously. David is gracious in victory. He does nothing to rub their noses in their defeat. He does not exact penalties or demand compensation. He forgives their rebellion. He makes a covenant with the leaders of Israel and becomes the God-anointed king of Israel.

David's wise rule lasts for 33 years.

Many people know all too well the temptation to gloat in victory. End-zone dances and post-dunk finger-pointing have become commonplace in sports. Whether we're scoring a decisive goal, celebrating the boss's adoption of our proposal or beating our competition for a major contract, we are tempted by the impulse to "rub it in." Powerful energy that could be used for building bridges and going forward is wasted by those who want to remind everyone who won and who lost.

Leaders with character rise above such impulses. They respect the convictions of those who have worked for a different outcome and incorporate them into the strategic plan. They show themselves to be the "bigger person." When we are driven by principles, we are not hijacked by our feelings. Our energy is dedicated to matters greater than petty reprisals.

Abraham Lincoln was frequently chastised for his leniency toward the enemy. "You must destroy your enemies," his generals hissed, "—not be nice to them!"

Lincoln famously responded, "And do I not destroy my enemies when I make them my friends?"

If you're still nursing a grudge, you likely have unfinished work to do. Or you may have a testimonial to recall, confirming the benefits you've experienced from forgiving someone. When we're at our best, we set our course by the larger vision of what we're put here to do. Leaders are guided by vision and principles. They forgive and are gracious in their victories.

Together, we can move forward freely, in order to shape a better future.

15

How Often Should We Forgive?

Then Peter came and said to him, "Lord, if another member of the church sins against me, how often should I forgive? As many as seven times?" Jesus said to him, "Not seven times—but I tell you, seventy-seven times."

Matthew 18:21-22

WE CAN MAKE the hard work of forgiving a bit easier if we understand what's involved in the dynamic of forgiveness. Yesterday we noted that the tribal leaders' speech to David was based on three crucial foundations of forgiveness: relationship, accomplishment and promise.

Let's look at these in more depth. Today we will focus on how these foundations help us in our relationships with others. Tomorrow we will see how they illuminate God's relationship with us.

First, it is through forgiving that we recognize our common humanity. Being human, we're all deeply related. We're all created of the same stuff: we all breathe, we all bleed, we all share human hopes and dreams, and we all find ourselves falling short of those dreams sometimes. The tribal leaders said to David, "We are your very own flesh and bone."

William Sloane Coffin was one of the most influential Protestant preachers of the late 20th century, serving for 10 years as senior pastor of New York City's prestigious Riverside Church. More than once he said, "If we are not bound to one another in love, at least we are one in sin, and that is no mean bond ... for it precludes the possibility of separation in judgment." In other words, we will all stand as one before God. We are not ultimately different from each other. Among the reasons: "No one is righteous, no, not one." (Romans 3:10)

We're all in this together.

If we begin to let go of the offense that separates us from a sister or brother, we can recognize our shared humanness and our similarities. We are—all of us—more alike than not. We are in no position to condemn. David, then, accepted the leaders' appeal by acknowledging their relatedness to him and to each another.

Second, it is in forgiveness that we must see and name what is positive about the other person. We move the focus from ourselves to the other: from our woundedness to the other's decency, gifts and accomplishments. We recognize that the other person has good intentions, has done praiseworthy things, and likely shares many of the values and goals that we do.

The tribal leaders said to David, "When Saul ruled over us, you were the one who led Israel out to war and back." Their appeal moves from "we are" to "you were," thereby encouraging us, too, to shift from "me" and "we" to "you." Our focus moves from ourselves to the other person. As the "good person/bad person" dichotomy begins to fade, we can acknowledge the other person's positive qualities. Forgiveness becomes a call to respect and value the other.

Just as the first foundation of forgiveness names a truth about the present, the second one names a truth about the past. We can say that, yes, we are united in having faults and failings; but the other has also shown his or her capacity to do what is good. We are likely to have been one in purpose. David hears that the tribal leaders prize his valor and share a desire for a secure Israel.

I once came across a particularly memorable quote in an Andy Capp comic strip (though there are many other variations). In this comic, the town vicar meets Andy coming out of a pub, and he chastises Andy for not coming to church. Andy retorts, to the vicar:

> *"There's so much good in the worst of us,*
>
> *And so much bad in the best of us,*
>
> *It ill behooves any one of us*
>
> *To find some fault with the rest of us."*

That quote nicely sums up the first two foundations of forgiveness. There is bad in us, and there is good in the other. Ultimately, what justification do you have for holding yourself above someone else?

Third, it is through forgiveness that we are pointed toward the future. It's about what's before us, not what's behind us. "The Lord told you, 'You will shepherd my people, and you will be Israel's leader.'" Notice how, in the tribal members' speech, there is a shift again—from "you were" to "you will." By forgiving, we also choose to look forward in promise instead of looking back in anger. This is an act of faith, trusting that God will work through each of us to bring forth a future that blesses us all.

David understands that the tribal leaders are pledging their allegiance to him. They are intending to put the past behind them in the hope and expectation that David will do the same and accept them back into his service. David does this, and he accepts and makes a covenant with his former enemies. Their reconciliation does not change the past, but it creates an opening for a brighter, stronger future.

Do these foundations speak to you in your attempts to speak out in forgiveness?

This isn't the only way to analyze forgiveness, of course. There are other ancient religious disciplines; many modern psychological and sociological protocols; and popularly published methods ranging from three steps to more than a dozen. There also is self-forgiveness and forgiveness that doesn't involve reconciliation between parties—for example, forgiveness of someone who continues to be dangerous or someone who has died.

Today's reflection isn't intended as the ultimate definition of the vast topic of forgiveness or the only prescription for reconciliation. But there is ancient wisdom we can glean from this story, from this exchange between David and the tribes of Israel. If these reflections on forgiveness strike a meaningful chord in your life, you should know that there are many forgiveness resources available that pastors, counselors and other professionals can recommend.

But—to put it quite simply—when I've been stuck in a grudge over the years, David's story has given me hope for forgiveness and reconciliation. We can see God's creative and healing power flowing through this story, resting on foundations that many of us can use in our own lives. I've often drawn on this wisdom myself.

So, how about you and that grudge you may still be nursing? Can God's gracious spirit lead you to a fuller embrace of this wisdom from David's life?

16

Nobody Does It Better

We are more than conquerors through him who loved us. For I am convinced that neither death, nor life, nor angels, nor rulers, nor things present, nor things to come, nor powers, nor height, nor depth, nor anything else in all creation, will be able to separate us from the love of God in Christ Jesus our Lord.

Romans 8:37-38

IN THIS THIRD reflection on forgiveness, we again turn to the foundations of forgiveness that were expressed in the tribal leaders' appeal to David. David hears their appeal, forgives their rebellion and welcomes them back as loyal followers. What are the foundations of this forgiveness which David grants? There are three: relationship, accomplishment and promise.

We've explored what deeper meaning the leaders' three simple sentences might have conveyed to David, as well as how they can help us to forgive. Today, let's look at how these three foundations describe God's relationship with us.

The key distinction here, of course, is that God's forgiveness is not a response to an appeal. God does not forgive us as an answer to our plea for mercy; on the contrary, God initiates forgiveness toward us. David forgives as a response to a particular appeal, but God forgives by pure grace. Our relationship with God changes only because of what God has freely chosen to do.

Let's deepen our understanding of God's forgiveness by using the same three foundations as our guidelines. We'll use some slightly different words, though—words with a stronger biblical pedigree—to express the same truth.

To replace relationship, accomplishment and promise, let's use covenant, character and commitment. The reality of our forgiveness rests on God's covenant with us, God's character and God's commitment to us.

First, the relationship God has established with us is a covenant. It is an unbreakable bond in which God pledges his fidelity, assuring us that we are never abandoned or forsaken. It is the deepest possible relationship there is or ever could be. There is nothing in all creation that will ever separate us from the love of God in Christ Jesus. (Romans 8:38-9) This covenant means that in everything that happens, God will work to turn it to the good.

We can be assured, then, of God's forgiveness through this covenant. To be forgiven through God's covenant doesn't depend on the sincerity of our appeal or God's mood at the moment. Instead, it's grounded in God's guaranteed, unbreakable covenant relationship with us.

Second, God's character is revealed in everything that God accomplishes or achieves. Everything that God does is, by definition, good. ("No one is good but God alone." Mark 10:18) It is contrary to God's very being to allow criticism, judgment or condemnation to have the final word. Through the eyes of faith, we can understand that God's actions—creation, covenant, commandments, corrections, Christ, church—all confirm that God's goodness never fails. Managers tell interviewers that past performance is the best predictor of future behavior. In the same way, we can trust God's character because we have *seen* it, through what God has accomplished for us.

Third, our forgiveness is grounded in God's commitment to an ultimate *shalom*—a healed and whole creation, a realm where every person lives in the right relationship in every possible way. That's the biblical vision. God is working to include you, me and everyone else in that final wholeness. God's trustworthy promise is that the merciful Jesus, the "son of David," will bring all creation to its fulfillment. The promise of forgiveness assures us that we will never be left behind, trapped in the captivity of our past mistakes. Forgiveness will reign. "Let us hold unswervingly to the hope we profess, for he who promised is faithful." (Hebrews 10:23)

Sometimes we use or hear the phrase, "That was unforgiveable." As a pastor there were multiple times when I would ask my congregation for sermon suggestions, requesting subjects they'd like to hear me address in a sermon. When I would ask, some parishioner would usually suggest a sermon on "the unforgiveable sin." From God's point of view, is there any such thing? Some may point out Jesus' reference in Matthew 12:31 and Mark 3:29, to the unforgivable "blaspheming the Holy Spirit"—and to parishioners who brought that up, I would always reply that while it's uncertain what he meant in that reference, it certainly is something far worse than saying, "Damn you, Holy Spirit!"

In fact, the entire message of the New Testament is built on Jesus' forgiveness of human sin. We can stand confidently on the biblical affirmation that there is nothing in all creation that can separate us from the love of God in Jesus. (Romans 8:38)

And whatever is meant by "blaspheming the Holy Spirit," that's clearly for Jesus to decide. One scholar, exegeting the meaning of that phrase, concluded, "If you're worried you might have committed this 'unforgiveable sin,' that's proof that you haven't." William Sloane Coffin, the Riverside preacher mentioned earlier, aptly said, "Guilt is your opinion of yourself. Forgiveness is God's opinion."

In our life together on earth, we can be assured of one thing: There is no offense against us that cannot be forgiven. There is no human behavior, ours or anyone else's, that deserves the label "unforgiveable." There are degrees of repentance, yes, and there are differences in our moral capacities to forgive, but there is never any justification to hold ourselves or anyone else out of mercy's reach.

If you are in a safe place, you might consider journaling or sharing an action or sin for which you've experienced forgiveness. Give thanks to God. If you are in a safe group, consider confessing an act or sin and let the group assure you of God's forgiveness. Hearing words of forgiveness spoken to you can be immensely powerful. For that matter, remember that you don't need to be Catholic to confess and receive absolution from a priest.

Alone or as a group, you may also want to perform a ritual of forgiveness, such as writing your action on a slip of paper and then burning or burying it. Read biblical words of forgiveness and assurance and insert your name into them, so you know they're intended for you.

God's covenant, character and commitment provides the assurance we need to claim and embrace forgiveness. This assurance gives us the foundation for forgiving others. If God has freely released us from the burdens of our humanity, we have no good reason to refuse the same to someone else.

God loves us. God forgives.

Nobody does it better.

Courage

17

David Dances Into Jerusalem

David went and brought up the ark of God from the house of Obed-edom to the city of David with rejoicing; and when those who bore the ark of the Lord had gone six paces, he sacrificed an ox and a fatling. David danced before the Lord with all his might.

Highlights from 2 Samuel 6:12b-17

FRESH FROM HIS reconciliation with the tribal leaders of the Northern Kingdom, David determines that he will make newly captured Jerusalem the capital of Judah and Israel combined. He intends that Jerusalem be both the political and spiritual center of his united monarchy. David leads a large group of warriors to the nearby village of Kiriath-jearim (also called Baal-Judah), where the Ark of the Covenant has been stored for 20 years. After a short layover in the house of Obed-Edom, David launches a festive parade to bring it into Jerusalem. He removes most of his clothing and accompanies the ark into the city with whirling, reckless abandon.

David's near-naked, ecstatic dancing has numerous explanations. He may be imitating the sacred dances of prophets, thereby claiming a prophetic identity. He may be co-opting practices more associated with Baal worship than with God worship. Other guesses abound, but his action is clearly daring and risky—one that requires bravery and nerve. Here, we're calling David's daring nerve "courage."

Courage is the *sine qua non* for leaders. No one leads by always playing it safe. Leadership is risky business, and leaders can be found in many places along a "risk continuum." We can put so-called "risk-inclined" leaders at one end, and "risk-averse" leaders at the other. Some leaders are drawn by risk: They're invigorated by daring actions that "cut against the grain."

They think that leadership, by definition, is moving ahead of the group, showing independence and challenging others to adopt the leader's reality as their own. The leader as an outlier, a visionary, a futurist and an innovator is intentionally destabilizing. In some ways, David's daring dancing fits here.

Risk-inclined leaders would do well to examine what compels them to disrupt the status quo. Some leaders thrive on chaos and on keeping others off-balance; others congratulate themselves for their bravery in consistently separating themselves from their organization. Some leaders cling to a variation of "Woe to you when all speak well of you" (Luke 6:26), finding virtue in the very act of fomenting discontent in their group.

Sean Martin, professor at the University of Virginia Darden School of Business, writes, "[Some leaders tend to] demonstrate self-confidence and comfort with risk-taking—and sadly, these traits may lead to the initial perception that they are impressive. But studies show that they are also more likely to disparage others, take more than reasonable credit, hog opportunities for themselves, engage in impulsive behavior and respond defensively to feedback."

By definition, risk-taking creates uncertainty. In an environment of uncertainty, it may be difficult to know just where a leader stands on any given day. Jeffrey Miller, in *The Anxious Organization*, writes, "A boss's displeasure is an objective survival threat to anyone who depends on a paycheck." Risk-inclined leadership can be dangerous.

Leaders on the opposite end of the leadership continuum are more risk-averse. These leaders usually understand that cohesion and stability are far more important to an organization's mission than disruption. Steady and reliable leaders free their organization from anxiety and uncertainty so that they can do their best work with confidence. Often, the culture itself contains so much "whitewater" that organizations value a steady steering hand.

Steadiness is contagious. When an organization has a clear mission and vision (as we discussed in Day 3 through Day 5), the leader who adheres to those principles promotes predictability, trust and focus. Predictability in an organization increases its effectiveness, as members can stay attentive to the mission without being distracted by anxious uncertainty. Effective leadership today consistently stresses mindfulness, collaboration, team-work, trust, relationship-building and other similar skills.

Successful risk-averse leaders are masters at analyzing changes in business and culture so that they can discern what choices they are avoiding—and the few changes they will decide to make. If challenging the status quo is called for, this kind of leader tends to carefully weigh the risks. This approach raises a whole host of questions among peers and co-workers, however. Is this leader avoiding change because of some higher principle? Is this leader exaggerating the consequences of risk? Is this leader flat-out afraid? If you are a risk-averse leader, you need people around you who are collaborative, trusting, clear-sighted and unafraid to speak openly.

My point is: Courage can be seen in both behaviors.

The risk-inclined leader shows courage by holding steady, restraining impulses, trusting the process and maintaining security. The risk-averse leader shows courage by stepping out, breaking the pattern, challenging expectations and disrupting the status quo. Rarely is effective leadership defined solely by one approach or the other. Rather, effective leadership is having the courage to act either way and dependent on the circumstances of a situation.

Where would Jesus fall on this continuum? Without pinning a label, we clearly see him exercise both aspects of courage in his ministry. True, the nature of his ministry was intentionally provocative: His divine mission was to overturn old assumptions about the world and inaugurate the kingdom of God. His confrontational entry into Jerusalem on Palm Sunday and his overturning merchants' tables in the temple are classic examples of a courage that challenged, provoked and antagonized.

Jesus also exercised restraint when restraint was more strategically effective. At the wedding in Cana, Jesus' mother urges him to do something when the wine runs out too soon. He replies, "Woman, what concern is that to you and to me? My hour is not yet come." Near the end of his life, while confronted by soldiers in a garden, he restrains a disciple from swinging his sword. In his final hours Jesus refrains from answering Caiaphas, resists the entreaties of Pilate, endures ridicule and punishment and allows himself to be crucified. All of this took courage.

Where, on such a continuum of courage, are you? What is your natural inclination? You might think of times when you've stuck your neck out for a good cause even though it would have been easier to stay silent. Or think of times when you've had to restrain yourself from speaking or acting impulsively, and saw the benefits of that restraint.

David was tasked with inaugurating a new future for a new nation. How do you judge his dancing? He clearly risked being provocative, even scandalous, in marking this bold beginning. The Greek philosopher Tacitus said, "The desire for safety stands against every great and noble enterprise." David chose scandal over safety as he inaugurated the new, united kingdom.

Want to spark a spirited discussion with friends? Start with this question: Is it better to be risk-averse or risk-inclined? Remind your friends that each direction may require a different type of courage.

We can pray, meditate and seek wise counsel to know, for ourselves, which form of courage we need.

18

David Disgusts His Wife

As the ark of the Lord came into the city of David, Michal daughter of Saul looked out of the window, and saw King David leaping and dancing before the Lord; and she despised him in her heart.

Highlights from 2 Samuel 6:12b-17

TODAY'S STORY MAY be one of the least-known chapters in David's life—unless you are one of the millions of Americans who admire the early American Shaker movement. One of the most beloved of all Shaker hymns brings to light this episode in David's life and rebukes Michal for her reaction to David. Although they are now fondly remembered and their furniture highly prized, the Shakers were despised in the early 1800s for breaking with Christian tradition and emphasizing worship through dance. The Shakers viewed David's daring, high-spirited dancing as the perfect way to "shake out" sins and energize a relationship with God.

Elder Issachar Bates wrote the tune that was proudly sung by Shakers for more than a century—and later became a folk classic, recorded by musicians such as Richie Havens, in the 1960s:

"Come life, Shaker life

Come life Eternal.

Shake, shake out of me

All that is carnal.

I'll take nimble steps;

I'll be a David.

I'll show Michal twice

How he behaved."

Leadership of an entirely new community is risky business and almost guaranteed to draw out negative reactions. The Shakers certainly found that as they tried to form their own version of a heavenly kingdom across the eastern half of the United States.

David found disgust very close to home. David's wife, Michal, sees David "leaping and dancing before the Lord" and is disgusted. With brutal honesty, our verse says—quite bluntly—that "she despised him in her heart." Michal regards her husband with contempt. She loses respect for him and scorns him. Why? Her reaction and the reasons behind it are ripe for speculation.

You may recall from earlier in David's story that we're told about Michal falling in love with him. However, never is it said that David loves Michal. So, we may be catching a glimpse of a marriage long troubled by unreciprocated love.

Chapter 3 of 2 Samuel names six wives of David; depending on the timeline of these marriages (also disputed), Michal may well have felt sidelined or ignored. Michal is, of course, the daughter of Saul—a king who was respected for his humility and modesty. David's dance is anything but humble and modest.

When the dancing is over, Michal confronts David at home and blasts him as "shameless" and a "vulgar fellow."

David fires back. "It was before the Lord, who chose me in place of your father and all his household … that I have danced." David delivers a pointed insult. Michal is caught in the middle of the old antagonism between these two men as she realizes that, to David, she will always be Saul's daughter. The fact that she remained childless all of her life (v. 23) may be either a judgment on her for her contempt or a judgment on David for never approaching her physically as a wife after that day.

The intentions behind David's dance are also fodder for speculation. Was David showing off? Was dancing so recklessly simply a vivid display of David's egotism? Was he arrogantly demonstrating that he was above the normal rules of decorum? Or was he selflessly acting like an ordinary commoner (a "vulgar fellow") before the ark of almighty God? Was he demeaning himself in order to elevate God?

Interestingly, this is how John Wesley understood David's dancing, and the story of David's twirling in public sparked a major shift in Wesley's ministry. Up until the spring of 1739, Wesley was a proper Anglican priest. He performed his ministerial duties within the confines of his Bristol parish. But that spring, riots around Bristol had risen to a fever pitch. Coal miners were taking to the streets to protest high food prices, low wages, poverty and discrimination. Revivalists such as George Whitefield saw, in the crowds of miners, rich opportunities to preach the gospel of salvation. Whitefield encouraged Wesley to leave the safe boundaries of his parish and join him in outdoor preaching.

In his journal, Wesley wrote, "I could scarce reconcile myself at first to this strange way of preaching in the fields, of which Whitefield set me an example on Sunday, having been all my life (till very lately) so tenacious of every point relating to decency and order, that I should have thought the saving of souls almost a sin if it had not been done in a church."

Yet through prayer, signs of providence and the encouragement of others, Wesley put the mission of Jesus Christ above the conventions of his tradition. Quoting David's rebuke of Michal in this very story, Wesley wrote, "At four in the afternoon I submitted to 'yet be more vile' and proclaimed in the highways the glad tidings of salvation." He noted that he was thinking of David's words in 2 Samuel 6:22.

Wesley was inspired by David's courageous dancing because he understood the story as David lowering himself, risking criticism and contempt, in order to elevate God. Giving honor to Yahweh superseded any concerns for dignity and propriety. Wesley followed David's lead and began to preach outdoors in roads and fields, risking contempt in order to share the message of Jesus Christ.

This is a pivotal moment in Methodism, as well as in American and European history. Methodism became known for "field preaching," for "going where the people are" instead of waiting for people to show up in church. Methodism's growth in America was rooted in its preachers' willingness to forsake the settled life in order to travel into the frontier and preach to American pioneers.

Being a Methodist circuit rider took courage.

"Doing a new thing" takes courage. The "new thing" often asks us to minimize our own needs in order to serve the greater mission of an organization. David inaugurated his new kingdom by putting the Ark of the Covenant—the presence of God—at the focal point of the new nation. We can debate how much ego was or wasn't in David's dancing, but he intentionally made God's ark the central symbol of a nation joined in covenant with God.

According to Patrick Lencioni, an American writer who authors books on business management, "For a Christian leader, this subjugation of self to mission is paramount, because the only reason to challenge a process is to serve Christ." David, of course, lived 1,000 years before Christ, but his challenge to "process" (the way things have always been done) was equally God-centered.

We may face a similar challenge to unite two parties under a new mission. We may be blending families or uniting a church. We may be combining work teams, integrating departments, merging companies or unifying a nation. What is paramount is the "subjugation of self to mission."

What is the highest good we're aiming to achieve? What within us balks at moving forward faithfully? What old ways do we need to challenge (and maybe even discard) in order to meet this new moment?

Where and when you are called to act with courage will be unique to you, but remember that you are likely to earn scorn. Keep in mind, however, an old adage: "Courage is simply fear that says its prayers."

God is with you.

Gratitude

19

David Says 'Thank You'

Then King David went in and sat before the Lord, and said, "Who am I, O Lord God, and what is my house, that you have brought me thus far? ... Because of your promise, and according to your own heart, you have wrought all this greatness, so that your servant may know it. Therefore you are great, O Lord God; for there is no one like you, and there is no God besides you, according to all that we have heard with our ears."

Highlights from 2 Samuel 7:1-29

AS SOON AS Jerusalem is established as the center of Israel, David wants to erect a temple in God's honor. Nathan assures David that this will please God, but that very night, God tells Nathan the opposite: It will not please him. Instead of *David* building *God* a house (a temple), God instead plans to build *David* a house (a dynasty). It is a massive and unexpected turn of events. David is overwhelmed. He retires to offer a long prayer of thanks.

His prayer involves two themes. The first part Walter Brueggemann names "deference." David prays out of his humility and awe: "Who am I, O Lord God?" Over and over David addresses God as "Sovereign Lord" and himself as "your servant." David is astounded at the generosity of God's promised loyalty, which causes him to remember the distance he has traveled—from obscurity on his family's farm to ruler of Israel, as God's chosen king. David is humbled and awed, self-effacing and deferential.

Awe walks hand-in-hand with humility. David expresses this humble awe in a psalm ascribed to him: "When I look at your heavens, the work of your fingers, the moon and the stars that you have established, what are human beings that you are mindful of them, mortals that you care for them?" (Psalm 8:3-4)

Overwhelmed by God's majesty to this day, we still honor God for including us in the magnificence of creation.

President John Kennedy, a lifelong sailor famous for his service in the U.S. Navy, kept on his desk a small plaque that contained lines from a poem by Disciples of Christ minister Winfred Ernest Garrison:

Thy sea, O God, so great,

My boat so small.

It cannot be that any happy fate

Will me befall

Save as Thy goodness opens paths for me

Through the consuming vastness of the sea.

Awe at the vastness of sea and sky leads to gratitude for times of safety and blessing. David is astounded and humbled at the sweep of God's kindnesses to him.

The second section of David's prayer is a doxology. It is pure praise. David takes himself out of the conversation to focus solely on God's being and God's deeds. Versions of the pronoun "you" dominate: your promise, your heart, your greatness. David moves from marveling at his relationship with God to marveling at and praising God alone.

Praise also walks hand-in-hand with gratitude. Being in the presence of God—or of anything that's majestic and magnificent—moves us to thanksgiving for simply being alive in such a moment. The Psalms consistently links praise and thanksgiving together:

- "Then I will thank you in the great congregation; in the mighty throng I will praise you." (35:18)
- "In God, whose word I praise ... I will render thank offerings to you." (56:10-12)
- "Enter his gates with thanksgiving, and his courts with praise. Give thanks to him, and bless his name." (100:4)
- "Praise the Lord! O give thanks to the Lord, for he is good; for his steadfast love endures forever." (106:1)

I once worked with a woman whose daughter was convicted of a misdemeanor and sentenced to 30 days in the county jail. On the morning that she would begin her incarceration, this woman gave her daughter a gratitude journal.

"What is this?!" the daughter screamed. "A gratitude journal? Do you think I'm grateful to be going to jail? What's wrong with you?!"

Her mother calmly replied, "You'll have a lot of time to think. This just asks you to write down five things each day you're thankful for. Just take it—use it if you want to."

Thirty days later, this woman picked up her daughter at the jailhouse door. The daughter had with her the possessions she'd taken in, including her gratitude journal; the journal now contained 150 different blessings for which she was thankful. Humility had led her to praise, which brought her to gratitude. That gratitude journal formed a new foundation for this young woman to go forward.

What sorts of things would you write in such a journal? In dark times— even in prisons of your own making—what can you be grateful for? Your list may have clear blessings and high spots: family, friends, opportunities. It may also contain disasters that ultimately led you to a better place of spirit: going to jail, hitting rock-bottom, being fired.

Garth Brooks has a lovely song called *Unanswered Prayers*, in which he remembers his adolescent pleas to God for things that didn't come to fruition—and yet he's moved to marvel at the shape of his current life and how much better he finds it. "I guess the Lord knows what he's doin' after all ... I thank God for unanswered prayers."

Can you "give thanks in all circumstances," as Paul exhorts in his letter to the Thessalonians? "This is the will of God in Christ Jesus for you." (1 Thess. 5:18)

David pauses at a key moment and is overcome with gratitude. Perhaps he muses as Brooks does: "I guess the Lord knows what he's doin' after all." Our roads with God have unforeseen switchbacks, stretches full of potholes and unanticipated vistas of beauty. Wise ancestors have taught us that the most important prayer in the world contains just two words: Thank you.

David's path forward will continue to be marked by triumph and blessing. Sadly, his gratitude and humility don't last long. Shortly after his night of prayer, David plunges back into the bloody business of war against nearby towns and armies. David is unfailingly victorious, though his triumphs don't continue to prompt gratitude.

But for a moment, here and now, David expresses his appreciation. He will learn that gratitude to God must be faithfully cultivated. As it was for David, so it remains with us.

Self-Control

20

David Succumbs to Temptation

It happened, late one afternoon, when David rose from his couch and was walking about on the roof of the king's house, that he saw from the roof a woman bathing; the woman was very beautiful. David sent someone to inquire about the woman. It was reported, "This is Bathsheba daughter of Eliam, the wife of Uriah the Hittite."

So, David sent messengers to get her, and she came to him, and he lay with her.

Highlights from 2 Samuel 11:1-27

DAVID'S BEHAVIOR WITH Bathsheba and Uriah marks his first personal and private crisis. Every other event thus far has been public and governed by openly political or military events. His anointing, his encounters with Goliath, Saul, Abigail and the tribal leaders, his dancing before the whole of Jerusalem, even his dialogue with Nathan prior to his prayer of gratitude—all of these have a public side.

This time the battlefield is not visible, like a house or a field or a capital square. The real battlefield is where desires and impulses roam and where guilt, deception, grief and regret all wander unrestrained. This battlefield is internal. David's psyche is alien territory for the warrior-king, and he fails miserably in his attempts to succeed here.

The story is simple and well-known. David is home in Jerusalem while his soldiers are out fighting. He strolls around his balcony late one afternoon and spies a beautiful woman bathing in her home some distance away. He stops. He stares. He stares some more. He summons his servants to inquire about her and learns that she is Bathsheba. David sends messengers to get her. They bring her to David, he forces himself upon her and then he sends her home. When Bathsheba later informs him that she is pregnant, David launches an elaborate cover-up that results in the death of her husband, Uriah.

For many, the challenge in reflecting on this story lies in our inability to see it with fresh eyes; a host of imagery and assumptions directly out of TV and Hollywood swirl in our minds when we hear about "David and Bathsheba." In fact, those three words are the title of a 1951 Technicolor blockbuster—one that even managed to shoehorn Goliath into its two-hour run time. David is played by Gregory Peck and Bathsheba is played by Susan Hayward. The leading actor and actress are approximately the same age, and the story is presented as an affair born of mutual attraction. Near the film's end, Bathsheba insists to David that she is not blameless in the doom that befalls David and that she, too, bears responsibility for their fate.

Some biblical scholars point out that Bathsheba utters no protest when David takes her to bed. Why doesn't she object, as Tamar did when her brother, Amnon, forced himself upon her? "No, do not force me," Tamar cries, "for such a thing is not done in Israel." (2 Samuel 13:12) Whatever Bathsheba may or may not have said is unknown. The text leaves her silent.

Between David and Bathsheba, the difference in age and status is significant. Bathsheba is the granddaughter of one of David's chief advisers and the daughter of one of David's soldiers, so a generational difference is likely. Biblical scholars have combed the Scriptures to assign proper dates to this event. Without going into great detail, choosing a middle range of approximate dates puts David at around 50 years old and Bathsheba at around 22. They are far from equals in age and maturity. Furthermore, he is royalty and she is not. He is powerful and she is not. There's no hint of mutuality in their meeting, and in fact, David has no idea who she is. David simply stares at her, sends for her, beds her and dismisses her.

In 1951 Hollywood, this may have seemed like a timeless, tragic love story. Today, we believe that this was rape. David raped Bathsheba.

This is the dark side of David's saga. It's a cautionary tale, an account of a gallant leader whose behavior is *not* to be emulated or copied. It exemplifies the "moral flabbiness" we read about on Day 7 in this book. That makes it an unusual entry in the chronicle of Israel's noblest leader. Yet our seeing the "clay feet" of such an outstanding man does, at least, make him more human.

All of us have the experience of being tempted to do something we shouldn't. Whether we pocket a candy bar at the drugstore, linger at a bar for "just one more" or say something to a co-worker we've determined not to say, we all know the tug of temptation. It's extraordinarily difficult to ward it off, which is why temptation is such a powerful and underrated foe. As soon as creation is finished (according to Genesis), temptation appears immediately. It is humankind's first and fiercest enemy.

St. Paul acknowledges as much in his famous confession in Letter to the Romans. He acknowledges sin's power to tempt by putting his personal struggles under the microscope. "I do not understand my own actions. For I do not do what I want, but I do the very thing that I hate. ... I can will what is right, but I cannot do it. For I do not do the good that I want, but the evil I do not want is what I do." (Romans 7:15f.) Temptation holds an alluring power to render us powerless. It's an agonizing part of being human.

Where are you most vulnerable to temptation? What enticements lure you most powerfully? To be human is to have "weak spots," and wise leaders don't deny or ignore them. Wise leaders learn to recognize their weaknesses and to know when "buttons are being pushed." Critical to maintaining your integrity is knowing your potential vulnerability to the appeal of alcohol, sex, drugs, money, flattery, risk—whatever.

Conversely, when have you successfully resisted the temptation to do something you knew you shouldn't? In Shakespeare's *Measure for Measure*, Angelo says to his companion, "'Tis one thing to be tempted, Escalus, another thing to fall." What has helped keep you from falling? What Bible passages, stories, memories or visions have given you strength in tempting times?

Are you part of a 12-step program, or do you have a loved one who follows the program? Now that you are two-thirds of the way through these 30 days, you could spark a spirited discussion with friends who know that system by asking about parallels between the 12 steps and the values we are exploring in this book. You may be surprised.

Of course, our story in 2 Samuel does not end with David's assault on Bathsheba. The tragedy only deepens. David tries to get Uriah to return from battle and sleep with his wife, hoping that her pregnancy will be attributed to Uriah. When that fails, he enlists Joab in a stealthy scheme to expose Uriah to enemy swords. Joab colludes, and Uriah dies.

All of these evils—lies, and even murder—cascade from David's failure to exercise one simple virtue, the fruit of the Holy Spirit: self-control.

Tomorrow we'll consider more deeply the spiral which pulled David down and the ways that God can help us maintain integrity. A clue comes from David's Psalm 37: "Take delight in the Lord, and he will give you the desires of your heart." (v. 4) David doesn't mean that God will simply agree to whatever you desire; rather, delighting in God can enable God to lift up within you the right desires and the right longings, so that your desire to live faithfully can win out over your desire to live impulsively.

Faithful living is not built just on good advice alone. Developing self-control begins with inviting God into the deepest recesses of your being, to the place where "soul and spirit, joints and marrow" meet. That space within you is God's alone.

As millions of 12-step followers will affirm, God can develop self-control in a receptive heart.

21

David Ignores Stop Signs

David sent someone to inquire about the woman. It was reported, "This is Bathsheba daughter of Eliam, the wife of Uriah the Hittite." So, David sent messengers to get her, and she came to him, and he lay with her … Then she returned to her house.

The woman conceived; and she sent and told David, "I am pregnant."

So, David sent word to Joab, "Send me Uriah the Hittite." And Joab sent Uriah to David.

Highlights from 2 Samuel 11:1-27

THE DIFFICULTY DAVID has in controlling his impulses is captured in one little word: So. It appears twice in our verses today. David walks around the balcony in the late afternoon and sees a beautiful woman bathing. He learns that she is Bathsheba. "So, David sent messengers to get her." David forces himself upon her, and later, she tells him that she is pregnant. Verse 6 states, "So, David sent word to Joab."

That little word appears again in verses 12 and 22, where it refers to subjects obeying superiors and implies the same automatic response to what precedes it.

The little word "then" plays the same role as "so"; it indicates that one event follows another, automatically and without pause. "Then [Bathsheba] returned to her house." Then David ordered Uriah to go home. Then David tried again by getting Uriah drunk. Then David ordered Joab to isolate Uriah on the battlefield.

David's unreflective impulses could have been stopped on numerous occasions. He did not need to keep staring at Bathsheba; he did not need to ask who she was; he did not need to send for her; he did not need to lay with her. David did not need to start a cover-up through Joab; he did not need to send Uriah home, either once or twice. The whole story flows from one action to another, without pause, as though David had no choice but to do as he did.

The tragedy of this story lies in how often that David stands at a moment of decision and ignores better choices—time and time again.

In psychological terms, this moment of decision is where a particular action or stimulus has ended and a response is pending. In some cases, the moment between stimulus and response is miniscule; Ivan Pavlov's classically conditioned dog learns to salivate at the first sound of a bell. We humans may have been conditioned to react to certain stimuli almost instantaneously. Yet in many situations, we have ample opportunity to get control of ourselves and choose our next steps carefully. We have free will, meaning that we have the freedom to choose our responses.

Is there a way to push apart the narrow space between stimulus and response? Can we ever make some space in what feels inevitable, so that we can exercise free will and choose our responses more wisely?

Viktor Frankl was an Austrian psychiatrist imprisoned by the Nazis during World War II. In his book *Man's Search for Meaning*, Frankl describes how he became aware that, while the Nazis controlled so much of his existence, their control over him was not total. Despite all the power that they had to control his environment and his body, he always had control over how he would respond. He could make meaning out of his experiences. He acknowledged that he was often left with "the last of the human freedoms": the freedom to choose response.

While in the camp, Frankl could choose hatred and bitterness—but that response wasn't inevitable. He could also choose endurance and hope, faith and love, purpose and discipline. Between stimulus and response, human beings have the freedom to choose.

How do we enlarge that freedom to choose? How do we begin to regain control over our automatic responses and bring them under the power of a higher authority?

One discipline that has helped me, personally, is mentally placing a question mark after the word "So."

When I'm tempted to do something unwise (send a scathing email, for example, to someone who has hurt me), I've learned that "So" can be a dangerous word because it allows for very little space between stimulus and response. But with a question mark—"So?"—it becomes an invitation to entertain different possibilities. Instead of thinking negatively—"That person wrote me a snide letter, so I need to write back"—my mental process can separate the stimulus and response by asking something different: "That person wrote me a snide letter. So?"

With that one-word question, my response is no longer dangerously automatic. I have signaled that discernment is needed—and, with that step, have allowed space for the freedom to choose how I will respond. That freedom, in itself, still may not solve the problem. Unfortunately, I sometimes choose to send the sharply worded email anyway, all the while knowing better. But the more often I can stop myself with a question, the more often I can create a space to choose more wisely.

The Christian leader has the same capacity to expand the space between stimulus and response, but I have never seen any evidence that pastors or lay leaders have any greater ability for this challenging task. We remember St. Paul's confession: "I do not do what I want, but I do the very thing I hate. ... I can will what is right, but I cannot do it."

Will power is never enough, even for devoted Christians. In that, we are all in the same boat.

This is why the faithful leader continually places her or his entire life before God. Practicing spiritual disciplines can bring us God's peace, as well as make us more aware of our "buttons"—the triggers that drive us to automatic reactions.

Reading and pondering Scripture is our heavenly parent's way of urging us to nurture some inner space. There are various lists of spiritual disciplines, but some of the most powerful practices are cultivating silence, practicing mindfulness, journaling reflectively and walking slowly. These and similar practices can help us expand the space between stimulus and response and choose more wisely.

As Deepak Chopra has said, "The space between thoughts is filled with unlimited possibility."

We can practice means of grace that develop cardinal virtues within us.

What spiritual habits and practices have been helpful for you in taming your impulses? Or, if this is a new thought, are you considering fresh steps in your life? You may know people who have come through challenges with their integrity intact. Do not be afraid to ask: "How did you do that?"

Consider this question: What possibilities might sprout between your thoughts?

As important as spiritual habits and practices may be, creating space to choose wisely isn't achieved just by our own efforts. We need outside help. Those places can be touched and shaped by the Holy Spirit. We can invite God to dwell in those spaces between stimulus and response, between impulse and reaction.

Need some encouragement? Remember the fruits of the Holy Spirit listed in Galatians 5:22: "love, joy, peace, patience, kindness, goodness, faithfulness, gentleness—and self-control."

Surrender

22

Nathan Confronts His Conniving Boss

Nathan said to David: "Now there came a traveler to the rich man, and he was loath to take one of his own flock or herd to prepare for the wayfarer who had come to him, but he took the poor man's lamb, and prepared that for the guest who had come to him."

Then David's anger was greatly kindled against this man. He said to Nathan, "As the Lord lives, the man who has done this deserves to die; he shall restore the lamb fourfold, because he did this thing, and because he had no pity."

Nathan said to David, "You are the man!" ...
David said to Nathan, "I have sinned against the Lord."

Highlights from 2 Samuel 12:1-15

NATHAN'S CONFRONTATION WITH David is perhaps the most stunning scene in all of David's story. It is a moment-by-moment account of a deceiver unmasked. The king who thought he could get away with his evil deed is cornered. Being called out by Nathan is the low point of David's life, and the narrator wants to make sure we do not miss the terrible accumulation of David's sins that has led to this moment.

The teller of the story spends a great many verses going over the details of David's act against Bathsheba, his subsequent plot to have Uriah killed, and even the detailed instructions of precisely how the news of Uriah's death should be conveyed to the king. Following this report and the proper period of mourning, David marries Bathsheba. Right upon the heels of this wedding, the prophet Nathan comes to David. It's unclear how much actual time has passed since Bathsheba's rape, Uriah's murder and David's marriage, but the story moves swiftly from one scene to another.

Nathan's allegory of the murdered lamb is richly detailed, with comments about the poor man's children and the little lamb's feeding habits.

The story is so compelling that David is enthralled in the tale and quickly condemns the rich man for his cruelty and selfishness.

Nathan pounces. "You are the man," he says. At that point, there is little breath lost between Nathan's uttered words and the denunciations and consequences he piles up on his sovereign.

David is overwhelmed to the point of simple, poignant surrender. "I have sinned against the Lord." But the confession is a heartbreaking, bottom-of-the-barrel experience for the powerful king. His shame cuts deep.

Commentators use harsh language to capture the emotional immensity and intensity of the moment. They have described this scene as "raw," "shattering," "devastating," and a time of "excruciating vulnerability." David is trapped and ruthlessly exposed. He is naked and ashamed, and his simple words barely convey his humiliation.

This devastating moment illustrates Abraham Lincoln's apocryphal quote of centuries later: "I have been driven many times to my knees out of the overwhelming conviction that I had nowhere else to go." David has nowhere else to go.

Perhaps you've got some Hollywood scenes swirling in your mind once again. In 1985, director Bruce Beresford's film *King David* gave us a more nuanced image of David than did the 1951 movie version. Nevertheless, this is a powerhouse scene in the film, a pivotal moment, as Richard Gere's David conveys shock, fear, shame, embarrassment and, ultimately, resignation. So much is packed into this simple and almost buried confession: "I have sinned against the Lord."

For most of us, rock-bottom moments are private (like a family substance-abuse intervention), but sometimes they are humiliatingly public (like the arrest of a friend or loved one). In recent years we've seen an increase in the number of executives, sports figures and celebrities held publicly accountable for behavior that once was overlooked. Deserved or not, we see far more public rituals of humiliation and embarrassment today than we did years ago.

We fight to avoid them—to hold off humiliation at all costs. Yet those who have hit bottom, those with "nothing left to lose," often describe these humbling experiences as the first step into a new life of radical freedom and authenticity. Surrender marks the end of self-delusion, the end of the phony façade and a halt to the incessant lying to oneself and others. It is the end of the pervasive fear of being found out and exposed.

More than 2 million people around the world are currently in Alcoholics Anonymous, which means they have started with Step 1: "We admitted we were powerless over alcohol—that our lives had become unmanageable."

Most of the great sages of the world have linked the death of the ego and the loss of illusions to the process of rebirth to authentic life. Jesus' saying in Matthew is typical: "If any want to become my followers, let them deny themselves and take up their cross and follow me. Those who want to save their life will lose it, and those who lose their life for me will find it." (Matthew 16:24-25)

This paradox is woven into the fabric of human existence. Every well-lived life has to confront loss, surrender, denial, sacrifice and renunciation. Seeking to avoid those crises is understandable; learning to accept them, even to welcome them, is the only way we will find true and satisfying human existence.

Of similar thought, the poet Maya Angelou wrote, "At 15, life had taught me undeniably that surrender, in its place, was as honorable as resistance, especially if one had no choice."

If we find ourselves in a situation similar to David's, here are several widely recommended principles:

- **Remain calm and thoughtful.** Don't lash out, don't be sarcastic or vengeful, don't justify or explain. Say less and ponder more. Keep it simple. More explanations and protests rarely help. Practice the virtues of patience and self-control. Be honest. "Let your yes be yes and your no be no. Anything more than this comes from evil." (Matthew 5:37)

- **Remember you are not alone.** There is no one who can condemn you who hasn't also experienced a regret in the past. "No one is righteous, no, not one," Paul wrote to the Romans. And remember Bill Coffin's quote from Day 15: "We are one in sin, and that is no mean bond ... for it precludes the possibility of separation in judgment." You are where others before you have been and others after you will come.

- **Trust that God will use this situation for something good.** It is never God's intention merely to break down or humble without also being ready to build up or exalt. It will not be immediately clear what the new outcome will be, but remember that "in all things God works for the good." (Romans 8:28) Maintain hope.

When in your life have you walked this path? What is the story of your surrender? Where do these words and stories resonate with you now?

Surrender is a life-changing moment. It is often, despite how it may feel, a life-*saving* moment, too.

23

David Submits to God

Have mercy on me, O God, according to your steadfast love;
according to your abundant mercy, blot out my transgressions.
Wash me thoroughly from my iniquity and cleanse me from my sin. ...
Create in me a clean heart, O God, and put a new and right spirit within me.
Do not cast me away from your presence, and do
not take your holy spirit from me.
Restore to me the joy of your salvation and sustain in me a willing spirit.

Highlights from Psalm 51

IN RICHARD GERE'S character's version, David begins with biblical text: "I have sinned before the Lord."

Then, he adds a line not in the biblical account, but very much in keeping with the meaning of David's surrender: "Do with me what you will, Lord."

David's words of surrender foreshadow the words of surrender Jesus spoke in the Garden of Gethsemane before his crucifixion: "Not my will, but yours be done." (Luke 22:42) These words also link us directly to Psalm 51, the psalm that tradition says has its origin in this very moment of confrontation and surrender. Perhaps this was David's prayer after Nathan had left him. It's worth a closer look.

David immediately launches into his submission prayer, not even pausing to set the context or praise God. He simply begins: "Have mercy on me, O God, according to your steadfast love; according to your abundant mercy, blot out my transgressions. Wash me thoroughly from my iniquity and cleanse me from my sin." (Ps. 51:1)

David offers no details about what seems to have prompted his prayer, but that helps Psalm 51 serve as a universally applicable lament for the widest possible variety of human transgressions. In all sorts of wrongdoing we acknowledge that we can feel dirty, contaminated and unclean, and we desperately need God's help. This is a basic human experience. We can understand why this speaks as powerfully to a congregation gathered in public worship as to a tortured soul offering private prayer.

This is followed by lines that are profoundly raw and honest. David's guilt haunts him, and he can't escape it. He knows that, although he has sinned against Bathsheba, Uriah and perhaps others, his actions are ultimately offensive to God. "Against you, you alone, have I sinned ... so that you are justified in your sentence." God clearly has the right to let the consequences of sin play out without interference, and David will not rail against God for whatever happens to him as a result of his evil actions. His propensity to sin has been a part of his life since birth—the human condition we all share. David is painfully candid and authentic.

The next section contains David's plea for God's forgiving activity to begin. Powerful verbs indicate the response that he, as a person of faith, can anticipate from a loving and forgiving God. "Teach me ... purge me ... wash me ... let me hear (i.e., "speak to me") ... hide your face ... blot out ... create ... restore ... sustain ... ." David pleads for this action, trusting that God doesn't need to be convinced. This is the reliable outcome of a prayer of confession.

The person of faith knows that to every one of David's pleas in Psalm 51, God answers, "Yes."

"Have mercy on me ..."

"Yes."

"Wash me thoroughly ..."

"Yes."

"Teach me wisdom ..."

"Yes."

"Blot out ..."

"Yes."

"Create in me a clean heart ..."

"Yes."

"Deliver me ..."

"Yes."

"Open my lips ..."

"Yes."

David's moment of surrender is simultaneously his moment of forgiveness and renewal.

The final section contains David's clear affirmation that this process of confession and restoration will change him. Having the slate wiped clean doesn't simply return him to the life he lived prior to calling for Bathsheba; no, he will abandon the old and put on the new. He will teach and bear fresh witness to God. His language will change. His intent will change. His behavior will change. The truly forgiven sinner becomes a changed person—what St. Paul later will call "the new creation." David testifies to the power of God to change people's lives.

David has much more ahead of him—more grief, more struggle, more victory, more wisdom. He will complete his reign wounded but wiser, because God keeps the promise that David will begin a dynasty. David's family line continues on, generation after generation, until our attention focuses on the singular "son of David"—David's Bethlehem-born descendant. This man will also surrender his life to God, praying "Not my will, but thy will be done," and then will go forth to inaugurate the final reign of life transformed: the kingdom of God.

Prayers of surrender form the doorway to a transformed life. Religions and social movements around the world have their parallel wisdom. Jews tell how years of slavery and wandering in the wilderness were the necessary pathway to the Promised Land. Christians tell of crucifixion that leads to life eternal, of a "Good Friday" that has to precede an Easter Sunday. The word "Islam" in Arabic means "voluntary submission (or surrender) to God." A Muslim is "one who surrenders."

The Alcoholics Anonymous model for substantial change is also grounded in the power of surrender. Its initial steps are an admission of powerlessness, a belief that restoration can come from a higher power and an act of surrender.

All of these and more are part of David's psalm. Its lessons resonate to this very day.

At the end of 2018, a powerful political figure fell in humiliation. The personal lawyer to President Donald Trump, Michael Cohen, had his well-woven layers of lies exposed by prosecutors in court. That autumn, Cohen pled guilty to charges of bank fraud, tax fraud, lying to Congress, violating campaign finance laws and other felonies. On Dec. 12, he stood before the judge at his sentencing hearing and uttered remarks that included the following:

"Viktor Frankl, in his book *Man's Search for Meaning*, wrote, 'There are forces beyond your control that can take away everything you possess except one thing, your freedom to choose how you will respond to the situation.'

"Your Honor, this may seem hard to believe, but today is one of the most meaningful days of my life. The irony is today is the day I am getting my freedom back as you sit at the bench and you contemplate my fate.

"I want to be clear. I blame myself for the conduct which has brought me here today, and it was my own weakness, and a blind loyalty to this man that led me to choose a path of darkness over light. … [N]o matter what is decided today, owning this mistake will free me to be once more the person I really am. … [I]t will be my life's work to make it right, and to become the best possible version of myself."

Whatever your personal politics, you should be able to hear clearly his admission of guilt, his honestly naming his behavior as "a path of darkness," his surrender to a higher authority, his readiness to face the consequences, the changes he anticipates, the promises he vows and the hope of freedom that sustains him. That courtroom appearance was a life-changing and life-saving moment for Michael Cohen. In this single moment, at least, he is worthy of our emulation.

Perseverance

24

Nevertheless, He Persisted

Abiathar came up, and Zadok also, with all the Levites, carrying the ark of the covenant of God. They set down the ark of God, until the people had all passed out of the city. Then David said to Zadok, "Carry the ark of God back into the city. If I find favor in the eyes of the Lord, he will bring me back and let me see both it and the place where it stays. But if God says, 'I take no pleasure in you'—here I am, let him do to me what seems good to him."

Highlights from 2 Samuel 13-19

THE STORY OF the revolt led by David's son Absalom is the longest single narrative in David's history, covering multiple chapters. In it we continue to see a chastened David. Gone is the self-assured warrior who slaughtered a giant, seized the throne and ruled with courage and gratitude. Now David is arguably in his 60s, an aging man still living under the post-Bathsheba judgment of God: "Now therefore the sword shall never depart from your house … I will raise up trouble against you from within your own house." (2 Samuel 12:10, 11)

The despondent tone of Chapter 12 is brightened by a brief reference to Solomon's birth and a successful campaign against the Ammonites (from present-day Jordan). Then the seeds of Absalom's revolt are sown, as Chapter 13 opens with another rape. This time it is David's son, Amnon, who rapes his half-sister, Tamar. Absalom is furious and filled with hatred for Amnon. He begins to plot his revenge for his half-brother's crime.

So begins more than a decade of resentment, hatred, fear and alienation within David's family. Two years pass before Absalom finally orders Amnon's death. Absalom then flees to the region of Geshur (in the southern Golan Heights) for three years. Joab coordinates Absalom's return to Jerusalem, and Absalom lives there for two years without even being allowed back into his father's presence. David eventually welcomes Absalom back with a kiss, and Absalom begins a four-year period of posing as the king's representative and judge.

We can easily imagine the years of seething anger, icy distance, bitter obsessing and murderous scheming wracking David's family. This would exhaust anyone, most especially a patriarch in his 60s! After four years of gaining favor with the people of Israel and a full 11 years after Amnon's attack on Tamar, Absalom sets his rebellion into motion. He aims to depose his father as king and seize the throne for himself. From this point forward (15:7f.), David displays a weary perseverance in responding to Absalom's insurgency.

Perseverance has been defined as "steady persistence in a course of action ... especially in spite of difficulties, obstacles or discouragement." David certainly faces a difficult and discouraging dilemma: Quash the rebellion and kill its leader, his son, or concede the throne and face exile (if not execution). But even with stakes this high, David never exhibits any of his old fire. Upon hearing that Absalom is gathering supporters to attack Jerusalem, the warrior's first command is to run away. "Get up! Let us flee, or there will be no escape for us from Absalom. Hurry, or he will soon overtake us!" (15:14)

David is clearly tired. He is described as weeping, weary and discouraged. He talks fatalistically, even apathetically, about whether God would have him win or lose. (15:24-26) He has been unable to give clear orders or make his objectives known (18:9-15), and even his closest advisers can't predict his reaction to news from the battlefield. (18:19f.) Inner conflict concerning goals in the campaign against his son inhibits him from taking strong action. The verbs associated with David throughout the narrative mostly describe him moving around: David comes, sets out, passes through, crosses and arrives. He even disappears from the story altogether for stretches of time. (16:15–17:20; 18:9-23)

Nevertheless, David persists. He is able to lead while dispirited and command while weary. Even with his energy running low, he plants his friend, Hushai, as a spy in Absalom's circle (15:32-37), he tolerates Shimei's taunting (16:5-14) and he makes personal decisions for his followers.

In one atypical moment, David displays a burst of energy. He assembles his men, forms them into battle divisions and assigns commanders to each one. The verbs in 18:1-5 are active: he musters, appoints, divides, speaks, listens (and considers) and orders. The king is back! He remains in camp while his men go forth and win a bloody battle, and the fate of Absalom is sealed.

It's fair to assume that David remembers God's promise of faithfulness. Recollection is a crucial discipline in times of perseverance. Remembering the promises of God and naming ways we have been uplifted by experiences of grace can empower us "to run and not grow weary, to walk and not grow faint." God's presence sustains us through our seasons of weariness.

When have you struggled with seasons of weariness? Have you had periods of opposition and struggle, when it was hard to summon the energy to address urgent issues? Maybe it was even hard to determine exactly what outcome you wanted, as in the weary response, "Whatever!" Sometimes the best we're able to do, as the cliché says, is just put one foot in front of the other. Are you able to remember previous experiences of God's grace and faithfulness? It isn't often easy.

My mother's mother suffered from what we now call bipolar disorder but what we then called manic depression. Grandma would have months-long cycles of high energy and overactivity, followed by an equally long slide into glum depression. We were aware of the cycles, but she wasn't. All she knew was that every time she got depressed, it was "the worst I've ever felt." As years passed she became less able to remember her earlier cycles, which could reassure her that her depression would eventually lift. Without the memory of having felt good not that long ago—or the memory of having felt her depression lift before—she lost hope. She could rarely recognize grace in her life.

St. Paul knew battle weariness and depression, too. His traveling ministry was constantly met with disappointment, opposition, criticism and violence. He frequently writes about not losing heart. To the church in Corinth he alludes to this discouragement in a letter, yet he assures them that God's grace will keep them persisting in their task. "[T]his extraordinary power belongs to God and does not come from us. We are afflicted in every way, but not crushed; perplexed, but not driven to despair; persecuted, but not forsaken; struck down, but not destroyed." (2 Corinthians 4:7-9)

There is an extraordinary power given to David that lurks beneath the surface of this narrative. Under his weary perseverance is a man hard-pressed but not buckling; confounded but not without hope; hounded but not abandoned; pushed aside but not giving up.

By the grace of God he nevertheless persists.

25

Hanging in There

For we walk by faith, not by sight. Yes, we do have confidence, and we would rather be away from the body and at home with the Lord. So, whether we are at home or away, we make it our aim to please the Lord. For all of us must appear before the judgment seat of Christ, so that each may receive recompense for what has been done in the body, whether good or evil.

Highlights from 2 Corinthians 5:1-10

PERSEVERANCE USUALLY IS only necessary in times of weariness. When we are not tired, perplexed or frustrated, we find it easier to maintain vitality at work and at home. If energy is given to us on a regular basis, our goals can usually be reached by maintaining a consistent pace of progress. Perseverance describes a virtue deeper than just maintaining one's ordinary routine, however. It's digging deeper for stamina in times of challenge.

According to business writer Kate Kurzawska, leaders often find their pace and perseverance challenged in four ways:

- Being disliked
- Balancing needs
- Staying motivated
- Staying focused

First, leaders will face criticism of their personalities, their style and their manner of doing things. If there is personal antagonism or jealousy within the organization, leaders may have to contend with distancing actions, passive-aggressive behavior and possible sabotage. The disliked leader still needs to put aside personal concerns, persevere in making difficult choices and do what is necessary for the health of the mission.

Second, every leader must balance the needs of the company and mission with the needs of the people involved. Policies should be fair and evenly applied across the board. For example, if lateness is tolerated for some but not for others, resentment will infect the company's spirit. Certainly, exceptions can be made—but that process of balancing can wind up with the unintended result of uncertainty and suspicion among colleagues. That's why consistency is an important value.

Third, disappointment and disasters are inevitable. A persevering leader keeps her "eye on the prize," always being willing to explore new solutions and solve unforeseen problems in a fresh way. It is often stated: "Everything looks like a failure halfway through." Perseverance that inspires others requires a consistent belief in the long-range worth of the project.

Fourth, keeping focus in the midst of a deluge of details is a critical leadership task. When the work gets complicated, it's easy to be tempted to focus on what's urgent and minimize what's truly important. Leadership requires staying committed to priorities and concentrating on moving forward.

During David's challenge from Absalom, he felt these same tests of his perseverance. He was disdained by Absalom and taunted by Shimei, son of Gera (16:5f.). He balanced the needs of Ittai the Gittite (15:19f.) with the mission of his troops. Throughout the entire campaign David struggles to balance his love for his son and his duty to Israel. The entire narrative is permeated by David's efforts to stay motivated and focused when both of the likely results—defeat and abdication or victory and Absalom's death— are tragic.

As we mentioned earlier, the apostle Paul also struggled to persevere in the face of opposition. In one section of his Corinthian correspondence, Paul writes of being afflicted and perplexed; in another, he writes of "groaning" and "longing" as he lives with the "burden" of pressing on. The passage 2 Corinthians 5:1-10 is an enlightening companion passage to the text describing David's weariness during Absalom's revolt. (Note: While we have the closing verses at the top of the chapter, it's worth having the New Testament at hand so you can see the full reading.)

Paul encourages the Corinthians to continue facing persecutions with perseverance and hope. This is their life now, but it will not be so forever. The "earthly tent" of the human body will end, but they have the

Resurrection hope of a "heavenly dwelling" (better translated as a "spiritual body") that will be theirs in the age to come. Paul insists that the Holy Spirit has been given as a guarantee, a "down payment" on this future reality, so that they can believe without reservation.

The final four verses, printed above, speak to Kurzawska's four common challenges of leadership.

Are you disliked? Are the opinions of others distracting you? Paul says, "We make it our aim to please the Lord." We're encouraged to do only that which honors and pleases God and to put human opinions aside. Keep the Lord in your sight.

Are you balancing multiple pulls and tugs as a leader? "Have confidence," he urges, "for all of us must appear before the judgment seat of Christ." Only God can perfectly balance every competing claim, but he has given you the spirit of wisdom and understanding. Be confident and use your best discernment.

Are you struggling to stay motivated? Paul says, "We walk by faith and not by sight ... so that each of us will receive recompense for what has been done." Your work is not in vain. You may not be able to see visible signs of progress, but have faith in the vision that was given to you by God. You will be rewarded for your persistence.

Similarly, are you trying to keep focused on what's important and not be overwhelmed by detail? Again, "Walk by faith and not by sight." Make decisions on behalf of the important and not just the urgent. Keep thinking "big picture" and move forward in expectation.

Do these verses speak to you? Small group discussions can help broaden our grasp of what discourages us, what wearies us, what challenges us. You might also identify other sources of wisdom, inspiration, encouragement and blessing that help you cultivate the virtue of perseverance.

In the early months of 2019, newspaper columnist Michael Gerson was hospitalized with depression. On the first Sunday in May he preached at the Washington National Cathedral, focusing his remarks on the challenge that depression brings to the human soul. Near the close of that sermon, Gerson noted: "Many, understandably, pray for a strength they do not possess. But God's promise is somewhat different: That even when strength fails, there is perseverance. And when perseverance fails, there is hope. And even when hope fails, there is love. And love never fails."

26

When to Hold 'Em, When to Fold 'Em

Then David and all the people returned to Jerusalem.
Highlight from 2 Samuel 12

BEFORE WE LEAVE this pair of opposing virtues—surrender and perseverance—let's ponder their relationship for one more day through a particular vantage point. This vantage point is presented to us in the chapter immediately preceding the story of Absalom's revolt.

In Chapter 13, Absalom's story begins with his half-brother's rape of their sister, Tamar. Absalom's rebellion, which tests David's perseverance, is in full swing by Chapter 15. David perseveres faithfully through the end of the narrative.

Yet the chapter that precedes the Absalom narrative, Chapter 12, is anchored by Nathan's accusation of David for the Bathsheba-Uriah affair. David abandons the cover-up of his guilt and surrenders with his confession: "I have sinned against the Lord."

In other words, Chapter 12 is a surrender story. The next chapter, Chapter 13, begins a perseverance narrative. In the Nathan-David story and in the Absalom-David story, surrender and perseverance are juxtaposed. Surrender is a quality of leadership, and yet so is perseverance—its opposite.

Let's look at these together. When should we surrender, and when should we persevere? When should we "hang tight," and when should we "let go"? When crises come, how do we know which road to take?

We've noted that surrender certainly gets "bad press" as a course of action in our culture. Surrender implies defeat, failure and dishonor. We're urged to never give up, to never surrender and to always "keep on keepin' on."

Yet a refusal to surrender is sometimes evidence of stubborn ignorance—of thinking too much of ourselves and the rightness of our action. We also mentioned earlier that programs like Alcoholics Anonymous only succeed when a person takes the major step to surrender. Surrender is the key to sobriety. All 12-step programs have surrender in some form as their primary step.

Most Americans know Kenny Rogers' signature song, *The Gambler*, from which I have borrowed the title for this chapter. What you may not know is that Rogers' 1978 hit was written by Don Schlitz, who has written dozens of other songs for country music stars. Schlitz had a very hard start in the business, and initially, he scrambled to survive. His *Gambler* song was recorded several times before Rogers turned it into a smash—but those earlier renditions were flops. Schlitz chose perseverance and, sure enough, the fourth recording by Rogers touched a nerve nationwide.

If you search through Schlitz's long list of lyrics, you will discover that he proclaims the need to know when to hold—and when to fold—in other songs as well. One was a hit for Tanya Tucker, about the need for flexibility in marriage. The song uses the metaphor of trees that bend, rather than break, in the wind:

> *Like a tree out in the backyard,*
>
> *That never has been broken by the wind.*
>
> *Our love will last forever,*
>
> *If we're strong enough to bend.*

From ancient scriptures to popular music today, we hear the sage advice that sometimes we need to persevere and sometimes we simply need to surrender.

So, how do we make that choice? Based on the wisdom from David's life, we can first consider questioning perceived rightness and morality. Remember that it was David's perseverance in a selfish and shameful goal that led to his collapse. To cover up his rape of Bathsheba, David exerted great energy and countless hours setting his schemes in motion. Yet as the proverbial walls closed in and God sent the prophet Nathan to confront him, David was left with few options outside of confession and surrender. There was no way on earth that David could justify what he had done before this man of God. At this point, further perseverance and denial would have been clearly immoral.

Would you have advised David to persevere in resisting Absalom? Or would you have suggested he surrender and let Absalom take the throne? If Absalom were not family, surrender could have meant that David was flouting God's will, since God promised the throne to David's household forever. However, since Absalom was his son, David could have surrendered and still kept faith with God's promise that "Your house and your kingdom shall be made sure forever before me." (7:16)

What do you think? For David, were both options morally and religiously acceptable?

Closely connected to the question of morality is the question of transparency. David's twisted goal of getting away with murder was a secretive one. No one else knew. David certainly had reason to hide his action from Bathsheba, but David also hid his reasoning from his trusted general, Joab. David's tenacious undertaking was done alone. If you follow this part of the narrative, it becomes clear that lack of transparency becomes a telling sign that it was time for David to surrender.

The same principle operates within AA. Drinking alone is a troubling sign. Hiding bottles, swigging mouthwash and making excuses are all signs that transparency is lacking and perseverance isn't the best course.

In his resistance to the rebellion, though, David's goals are clear. This is a topic well worth discussing. What was David's strongest motive? Was it his ambition to rule again for the good of Israel? Or, at that point, was it a sign of his own overwhelming desires?

My interpretation of the story leans toward seeing David as neither shameful nor purely selfish in wanting to retain power. Among the evidence for this conclusion is that David had no shortage of soldiers, helpers, admirers and assistants. One of the small, often-overlooked details in the passage spanning chapters 12 to 19 is the brief scene at the end of Chapter 12, in which David's army is campaigning against the Ammonites and, at a key turning point, David needs to "gather all the people together" to defeat the foes. The record says that he was able to do that effectively and, at the end of that campaign, "David and all the people returned to Jerusalem."

Throughout this extensive narrative, David continues to attract the strong support of men and women. There was a clear public good and not merely a private good, which David makes clear. That transparency enables David to welcome others and their assistance.

When you feel comfortable engaging others or welcoming offers of help—or at least noticing and acknowledging those who want to join with you—this can point you toward perseverance.

There are so many common questions we face throughout our lives. Should I continue with chemo, or just surrender to cancer? Do I keep knocking on door after door for this cause, or do I throw in the towel? Do I keep funding this project, or cut my losses? You may feel it's time to surrender. There are no surefire, five-step discernment models that can make these tough choices for you, but one truth is abundantly clear: If you're surrounded by friends and helpers, you'll get more wisdom than you could find alone. For more than three centuries, prayerful community discernment has been a bedrock of the Quaker movement.

At crucial moments, David himself chose both holding and folding. In his confrontation with Nathan, David knew he could no longer hold 'em; he had to fold. But in his resistance to his son's insurrection, David could perhaps have gone either way. He chose to hold 'em—to resist and persevere.

Just as the lyrics of *The Gambler* don't spell out the conditions for perseverance versus surrender, neither does the Bible. But David's experience invites us to ask the right questions: questions about morality, transparency, secrecy, selfishness and the quality of our companions.

Since both surrender and perseverance are critical virtues for leadership, it proves that leadership is not a science, but an art.

Calmness

27

David Keeps His Cool

Shimei shouted while he cursed, "Out! Out! Murderer! Scoundrel! The Lord has avenged on all of you the blood of the house of Saul, in whose place you have reigned; and the Lord has given the kingdom into the hand of your son Absalom. See, disaster has overtaken you; for you are a man of blood." …

David said to Abishai and to all his servants … "Let him alone, and let him curse; for the Lord has bidden him."

Highlights from 2 Samuel 16:5-14

THIS IS A scene from early in David's long flight from Absalom and his men. David's composure in this story is quite remarkable.

Absalom heads southwest to Hebron, ostensibly to worship God at this sacred site, but he gathers his followers together while he's there and launches his rebellion against David. David hears that Absalom is coming back with a huge force of soldiers, and he immediately gathers his officials and abandons Jerusalem. David's group passes the Mount of Olives and continues northeast a few more miles, arriving at the town of Bahurim.

His welcoming party is a disgruntled relative of King Saul, named Shimei. Shimei greets the fugitive king and his soldiers with handfuls of stones and torrents of curses. Just a few miles back, David was weeping his way up the Mount of Olives; that emotion has barely passed before he's being taunted and insulted.

Shimei is a provocative antagonist. "Out! Out! Murderer! Scoundrel!" he screams. The Hebrew epithet translated as "murderer" is elsewhere translated as "butcher," "man of blood" and "killer." Shimei accuses David of perpetrating violence and death. He's primarily blaming David for Saul's demise ("the blood of the house of Saul," v. 8), though news about arranging Uriah's fate may also have made its way to Bahurim.

The second insult, here translated as "scoundrel," has also been translated as "criminal," "rogue," "despicable one" and "good-for-nothing."

Shimei's literal insult is "son of *belial*," with *belial* being a compound Hebrew word from *belli* (without or lacking) and *ya'al* (to have value). "Worthless" is a good translation.

These are dangerous insults for a commoner to hurl at a sovereign king surrounded by soldiers!

And, there's more! In addition to words, the physical act of throwing rocks and dirt has symbolic power. This action carries meanings ranging from denigration ("You are like dirt") to dismissal ("You mean no more than dirt") to wishing death ("I will throw dirt on your coffin"). In an already somber and tense atmosphere, Shimei's affront is like throwing a match into a gas-filled room.

As we might expect, Abishai—the king's nephew and bodyguard—reacts explosively. He wants to decapitate Shimei. "Let me go over and take off his head," he says. Abishai's response is immediate and near-instinctual, similar to the immediate, unreflective responses we discussed in the David and Bathsheba story.

David, however, responds with amazing calm. He manages his anxiety and emotions skillfully. A sharp and brutal reaction from David would be understandable, but his calmness and focus see him through this time of intense abuse. These are key qualities for a leader, especially as David is responding to such a challenge in the presence of his followers.

In his demeanor and speech, David exemplifies what has been called "resilient leadership." Resilient leadership is a way of approaching leadership based on the groundbreaking work of Murray Bowen, a psychiatrist, researcher and family therapist at the Georgetown University Family Center in the last few decades of the 20th century.

In a nutshell, Bowen took the family as his basic unit of study—not just the individual with symptoms, but the entire family cluster. He observed how the behaviors of each person in the family maintain the dysfunction of that family. Problematic behaviors in one or more individuals reinforce and lock in dynamics that consciously or unconsciously resist change.

Instead of identifying any one person as being "the problem"—around whom the family's attention would revolve—Bowen coached the most motivated person in the family to behave differently. New behavior—calmness instead of blame, for example, or humor instead of despair, or independence instead of acquiescence—would cause shifts in the family's way of operating. If that new behavior could be maintained in the face of pressure to change back, the entire family would slowly begin to function in a more thoughtful and less reactive way.

Students of Bowen (e.g., Ed Friedman, Roberta Gilbert, Peter Steinke, Ronald Richardson, Robert Duggan) have applied Bowen's work to organizational leadership and have developed some powerful insights into how a leader's ability to function in a mature and thoughtful way "ripples" down through the entire organization. Their writings can introduce an organization's leaders to key ideas such as triangles, over-functioning and under-functioning, regulating anxiety, self-differentiation and more.

Calmness—the value we will be exploring for three days—is a virtue associated with patience and temperance. So, first, consider the most common threats to these values that you see in your daily life. Managing one's personal anxiety is the foundational task of a leader, so it's helpful to know what raises your anxiety. Is it taunting or insults? Is it the prospect of failing?

Again, you are not alone! Many of us get anxious over losing control, being wrong, getting lost, being embarrassed or dealing with strong emotions like anger and sorrow. It is crucial for us to understand what "pushes our buttons" and where our emotional vulnerability is the most raw.

University of Virginia head basketball coach Tony Bennett, who led his 2018-2019 team to the NCAA national championship, had an intuitive understanding of a key concept in resilient leadership. Bennett had a mantra to keep his players focused when a game seemed to be slipping out of hand.

"Calm is contagious," he preached. The Cavaliers learned not to panic when they were behind. Coaches, assistants and team captains remained calm and steady in even the closest games. The team's leaders helped all of the players stay focused and composed the entire way to the championship.

Both David and Jesus faced trying times of insult and blame. "Be not anxious," Jesus urges us. Similarly, David remained calm in the face of Shimei's insults. We grow in character as we take to heart the same Holy Spirit that guided them both.

28

David Sets a Boundary

Then Abishai son of Zeruiah said to the king, "Why should this dead dog curse my lord the king? Let me go over and take off his head." But the king said, "What have I to do with you, you sons of Zeruiah? If he is cursing because the Lord has said to him, 'Curse David,' who then shall say, 'Why have you done so?'"

Highlights from 2 Samuel 16:5-14

THIS PENULTIMATE VIRTUE in our 30 days—calmness—is such a challenging goal that we are devoting three days to these reflections. Let's start by remembering the fury of the initial challenge to David as he is confronted by Shimei.

"Out! Out!" Further insults, both verbal and physical, cascade after these words.

At this point in David's life, many people despise him for some of his painfully public deeds (and perhaps also for some of the secrets about him that are emerging). In his retreat from Jerusalem, David is in the heart of his homeland. Long-buried family anxiety erupts when David appears in front of Shimei in person—and the furious barrage erupts!

Abishai, a commander from a military family, flares quickly. He's equally susceptible to the anxiety of the moment and is quick to draw his sword. We can imagine him thinking, "Just say the word, David, and he's a dead man."

David quickly cools Abishai's hot temper. "What have I to do with you?" he asks—in essence, saying, "This doesn't concern you, Abishai. It's none of your business."

This scene is an intense example of anxiety erupting and then being lowered by an experienced leader. As we saw yesterday, anxiety is a key concept in Bowen's theory and in the practice of resilient leadership.

Anxiety is an ever-present emotional state in all of us that often sparks action. When managed well, it joins with a leader's clear thinking and personal convictions in order to enable one to speak plainly, steadily and inspirationally. When not managed well, anxiety can spiral out of control and drive leaders into increasingly damaging and dysfunctional behavior.

Managing one's personal anxiety, which David does well here, is the foundational task of a leader. Managing personal anxiety is, in actuality, a critical task for every member of any organization, including the family unit.

Yet understanding how this is done is far more complex in practice, even in theory, than it may seem. Bowen's theory embraces insights into human anatomy, brain function, animal behavior, family dynamics, birth order, interpersonal psychology, leadership theories and more. For our purposes here, we'll focus on how David stays calm: by managing his anxiety, setting boundaries and focusing on his principles. This is work that Bowen and others explore under the concept "differentiation of self."

Abishai, for example, seems unable to manage his emotions very well. Shimei's taunts and insults trigger his emotional urge to react physically. Though not directed at him, Abishai rankles at Shimei's disrespect of David. This stimulates his "fight-flight" response, which Bowen locates in the amygdala, the most "primitive" part of the brain that is the source of our automatic survival impulses. Abishai is immediately roused to fight. He calls Shimei a "dead dog" and impatiently awaits David's word to behead him.

The amygdala is the part of the human brain that regulates fear and propels survival behavior. If you suddenly are confronted by a raging bear or something else that puts you in clear and present danger, your amygdala is your friend. It will disengage rational thinking and propel you to immediate action—and, we hope, to safety.

Most of us don't face an angry man screaming insults and throwing rocks at us. Nevertheless, our amygdala can kick in with instinctive and almost uncontrollable reactions. A nasty look raises our blood pressure. A slammed door instigates a vicious argument. A simple phrase is interpreted as "fightin' words." The amygdala "hijacks" our brain and separates it from calm, rational thinking.

In Bowen's theory and resilient leadership lingo, Abishai's reaction is called an "amygdala hijack." Whatever Abishai's personal story may have been—family history, boyhood bantering, childhood traumas, reasons for becoming a soldier, extensive military training—a stranger's provocation immediately triggers his willingness to kill.

David, by contrast, manages his emotions very well. His speech in verses 10-12 reflects effective leadership that is congruent with the resilient leadership approach grounded in Bowen's theory. He controls his anxiety and remains thoughtful and unruffled.

David's second approach is to set boundaries. He keeps the issue focused without allowing another's agenda to distract him. He calmly defines both the issue and the people involved.

Note that David's first words are "What have I to do with you?" He makes it clear that these insults and provocations are not aimed at Abishai. David sets a firm boundary around what is his issue and what isn't, and he stops Abishai from involving himself. He addresses Abishai in the plural ("you sons of Zeruiah"), seemingly with exasperation, and implicitly refers to Abishai's brother, Joab, who also offered David military service (and maybe to Abishai's other brother, Asahel, also a military man). It's unclear whether David is thinking of matters in the past that have involved the brothers or if he's simply marking off a matter that is his and his alone.

Third, calm leaders keep focus on basic principles, convictions and beliefs. Leaders stay true to their values. David has a core belief that God is present in all of his interactions, and this comes through in his words.

David actually suggests that Shimei's abuse might be God's will. "If he is cursing because the Lord has said to him, 'Curse David,' then who shall say, 'Why have you done so?'" David's faith enables him to consider that God might be behind Shimei's outburst; Shimei may not be David's enemy after all, but instead a messenger sent from God. David reiterates this thought just a few words later with even firmer confidence: "The Lord has bidden him."

In the process of hearing himself speak, David has moved from possibility to probability to perhaps even conviction. Shimei is here because of God's direction. This belief in the sovereignty of God is one of David's bedrock principles.

Have there been times when you've cooled other tempers and defused a situation? Or maybe you've been directly provoked yourself and somehow were able to remain calm. Have you had times when setting boundaries and staying out of someone else's business (or keeping them out of yours) has helped?

Are there principles in your life that have kept you from "taking the bait" when you were provoked? When have you brought calmness to a volatile situation?

Tomorrow we'll conclude our reflection on how David managed his anxiety and kept calm in the face of derision. This calmness, this being able "to keep your head," is essential to leadership.

29

David on the Balcony

David said to Abishai and to all his servants, "My own son seeks my life; how much more now may this Benjaminite! Let him alone and let him curse; for the Lord has bidden him. It may be that the Lord will look on my distress, and the Lord will repay me with good for this cursing of me today."

So David and his men went on the road, while Shimei went along on the hillside opposite him and cursed as he went, throwing stones and flinging dust at him.

Highlights from 2 Samuel 16:5-14

TODAY WE CONCLUDE this penultimate reflection on the value of calmness. In this, we must ask a crucial question: What defines calm leadership?

Yesterday, we considered three determinants of calm leadership:

1. Calm leaders manage their anxiety.
2. Calm leaders set boundaries.
3. Calm leaders focus on principles, convictions and beliefs.

Today, let's think about three more determinants that we can draw from the remaining words of David's response.

First, calm leaders look at the big picture. Just as focusing on clear boundaries and basic principles helps us to think more clearly, so clear thinking enables us to gain perspective. We can discover broad patterns, as though we are looking down from a balcony to a dance floor below. From that vantage point, we can discern more clearly the clusters, steps and directions of the dancers.

In taking a "balcony view," as public leadership expert Ronald Heifetz and others recommend, leaders are less likely to remain so focused on the small details close at hand that they end up banging into other participants. The real question comes into focus: "What's going on here?" Standing too close to the action makes even the smallest detail seem abnormally large.

A balcony perspective helps us put smaller events into a larger, more useful picture.

David can see a larger pattern in the people who are angry at and opposed to him. He understands Shimei's anger. "My own son seeks my life; how much more now may this Benjamite!" Some translations add the phrase "one of my very own children" after "my own son." The phrase "one of my very own children" is missing from many translations, but it translates an emphasis in the Hebrew text that adds poignancy and depth to David's plea.

It made sense to David that Shimei would despise him. Saul's clan had harbored bitterness toward David for years, while Absalom's disgust was more recent. Knowing that kinship and family ties weren't enough to restrain even his own son's hateful impulses, David could easily understand Shimei's animosity. David's clear perspective helped him maintain some objectivity.

Great leaders usually can discern the bigger picture—or, at least, that's the focus of their discernment when challenges arise. Why are we suddenly anxious? It's easy to answer that question with the nearest evidence: A rude man is throwing stones! Effective leadership involves a deeper, or perhaps higher, view of the entire context.

Second, calm leaders can let opposition have its voice. We don't need to automatically squelch or prohibit opposing points of view. "Let him alone, let him curse" encapsulates David's calmness and self-management. David respects boundaries and is able to let Shimei do what he needs to do. He understands that he can let an adversary—especially one who may be bringing a holy rebuke—still have his say. Silencing Shimei could easily provoke more hatred toward David from Saul's clan.

In his oft-quoted poem *If*, Rudyard Kipling elaborates on life's challenges to our emotional maturity. He uses the idea of "manhood" as his ideal, but we can easily understand that he was encouraging us to walk toward strength of character and integrity of soul whatever our gender. Remember the opening lines?

If you can keep your head when all about you

Are losing theirs and blaming it on you,

If you can trust yourself when all men doubt you,

But make allowance for their doubting too ...

David can allow Shimei and Abishai the experiences of reactivity and blame. He can regulate his emotions enough to calm the jittery warrior and let the raving Shimei have his say. Shimei doubts David's virtue and nobility and proclaims his alternate view passionately. David can allow Shimei his voice but still be ready to press on.

David also recognizes that, to the extent Shimei might be speaking God's judgment, God would not have sent such an insulting messenger to a completely holy and innocent man. There is indeed blood on David's hands. He must acknowledge that his failures were not merely private ones; his shortcomings, whichever ones might be on Shimei's personal list, are public knowledge. David may tolerate Shimei's scorn even as a public price to pay, a necessary penance for his guilt.

Third, calm leaders remain positive and optimistic. Resilient, principled leadership enables one to "fight the good fight" with buoyancy and hope. This attitude enables us to look for what is good and life-affirming in even the most challenging of crises.

"Perhaps the Lord will repay me with good for this cursing today." David expresses a familiar truth for the Israelite people: If God is ever behind hardship, God always follows with mercy and restoration. First one endures the wilderness, then God opens the Promised Land.

Remember that Joseph said to his brothers, "You meant evil against me, but God turned it to good." (Gen. 50:20) God is a redemptive God who seeks always, despite painful moments, the best for humanity. Judgment is never the final verdict. David's basic hope also comes through in a psalm credited to him: "God's anger is but for a moment; God's favor is for a lifetime. Weeping may linger for the night, but joy comes in the morning." (Ps. 30:5)

David consistently lives and leads from a place of hope.

Put yourself in David's place for a moment. Where have you sought out the big picture or worked to put a conflict in perspective? When have you allowed people space to share opposing views? Where can you embrace and radiate long-term hope? What opportunities might you have to project hope in days to come?

Nurturing the virtue of calmness, an expression of the classical virtue of temperance, magnifies our effectiveness as leaders. Steadiness spreads. Calm is contagious. Hope is catching. In Jeffrey Miller's words, "A leader's composure is tremendously reassuring to followers. It flows down the chain of command as inexorably as Niagara Falls. Steadiness at the top steadies an entire organization."

Or, as John's Gospel tells us, "Jesus said to them, 'Peace be with you. As the Father has sent me, so I send you.'" (John 20:21) What good leaders receive can be made visible in our relationships with others. The more we express and live from the best of our character, the more we influence the groups with which we live. Character can shape the world for the better.

God's peace, God's calm and serenity, is infectious—through you.

Justice

30

David's Last Words

Now these are the last words of David:
The God of Israel has spoken, the Rock of Israel has said to me: One who rules
over people justly, ruling in the fear of God, is like the light of morning, like the
sun rising on a cloudless morning, gleaming from the rain on the grassy land.
Is not my house like this with God? For he has made with me
an everlasting covenant, ordered in all things and secure. Will
he not cause to prosper all my help and my desire?

Highlights from 2 Samuel 23

OVER THE YEARS, many books have focused on the final words by—
and words about—famous men and women.

Samson's final words are unforgettable: "Let me die with the Philistines."
Hollywood captured the scene more than once as the seemingly defeated
Samson pulls down the pillars of the Philistine temple.

Or, "You, too?" Caesar can't believe that his friend Brutus is part of the
plot against him.

"It is finished." Christians recall these words of Jesus every year.

We are amazed at the ironies! Jefferson's last words were: "Is it the
Fourth?" He was apparently pleased that his last day in July 1826 coin-
cided with his nation's birthday.

We hope that last words carry a lifetime of wisdom compressed into a
short sentence, or that they somehow encapsulate the dying person's legacy. We enjoy finding out whether the last words people choose to say in
this life are memorably profound or amusingly ordinary. They're usually
closer to the latter than the former.

There are also long lists of mythic last words. Utterances like "rosebud"
in *Citizen Kane* certainly were not the final words of the movie's infamous
model, William Randolph Hearst.

The Scriptures actually contain two accounts of David's "last words." The
first is today's passage, 2 Samuel 23:1-7. You will find the second version in

1 Kings 2:1-9. (And you'll find many more suggestions for further reading in the section at the end of this book, titled *Care to read more?*)

The Kings passage contains a theological formula foreign to David (vs. 3-4) and some petty score-settling (5-9). They're ordinary words—too predictable. The 2 Samuel passage is a much more honorable and profound epitaph for this great figure of history, so let's look at that.

David does recap some of his life story in these verses. He summarizes his identity in the opening verse, his work in the middle ones, and his legacy in the closing section. This is the way he sees his life as a whole.

David roots his identity in the ways that he was acted upon (verse 1): He was "exalted" and "anointed" by God. David believes that his identity has been received, not self-made. He was not "the master of his fate … the captain of his soul," but instead one who was chosen, blessed and guided by God's mysterious initiative. The final phrase, here translated "the favorite of the Strong One of Israel," is confusing in the original Hebrew and has been translated many ways, including "the hero of Israel's songs." Both translations are truthful renditions of the Hebrew.

Likewise, David's legacy (verse 5) is grounded in God's mysterious initiative. God's covenant with him and his descendants has made all the difference. God's covenant gave him a lifelong security, a foundation of trust that will long outlive him. God was faithful in every promise.

The translations carry some important theological subtlety. The NRSV translation of verse 5 can be slightly misleading. "Is not my house like this with God? For he has made with me an everlasting covenant" doesn't link David's justice and God's covenant; it simply lets them stand side by side. That translation uses a negative to elicit an affirmation. ("Is not my house … ?") An even more misleading translation is the New International Version (NIV), which offers "If my house were not right with God, surely he would not have made with me an everlasting covenant…." That translation uses a double negative and erroneously implies that God established a covenant with David because David was right with God. The opposite is true: David is right with God only because of God's covenant on his behalf.

The King James translation is perhaps most accurate: "Although my house be not so with God; yet he hath made with me an everlasting covenant … ." Despite David's sins and wrongdoing, God initiated and kept a faithful covenant with him. Whatever order, security and salvation were in

David's life, they flowed solely from God's undeserved grace. To whatever extent David's rule brought justice and light, the honor was solely God's.

David summarizes his primary work—speaking and ruling—in the middle verses (2-4). At his best, David spoke God's wisdom. God worked through him as messenger and mouthpiece, a role that was grounded in David's consistent worship of God as well as David's study and singing of God's message. David obviously does not just spout Scripture or pepper his conversation with chapters and verse. David's expressions—including his timeless masterpieces in the book of Psalms—give God glory and praise for whatever wisdom and direction he spoke to his people.

For the heart of these final words, we can easily substitute "leads" for "rules over." "Ruling over justly" is leading with fairness and integrity. The human leadership that God blesses is fair, humble and just. It honors human beings and treats them evenly and impartially. It is uplifting and inspiring. It seeks to lead, as in Lincoln's memorable phrase, "with malice toward none, with charity for all, with firmness in the right as God gives us to see the right ... ."

This is virtue-driven, character-driven leadership. Such leadership listens deeply, considers thoughtfully, decides wisely and acts humbly. The similes in the text of dawn and rain emphasize that the purpose of leadership is to bring hope and fruitfulness. Like sun and rain, leadership that is just awakens possibilities, encourages hope, brings light, instills warmth, cultivates tender beginnings and spreads vitality throughout its area of influence.

There are abundant examples of companies, governments and families in which the opposite is true. Wherever an organization is chaotic, insecure, cold and competitive—or where the fear of making mistakes is high—there is a failure of leadership. Where suspicion runs rampant, family members distance themselves from one another, parishioners plot parking lot coups, employees protect their turf and administration appointees suffer high turnover. In all of these cases there is a failure of leadership. And that failure relates directly to the degree of humility and fairness in the leader.

To put it bluntly: This is an issue of character. In six words, that has been the core theme of these 30 days.

Failures of leadership may have roots that run deeper than the current man or woman at the helm. Cultures aren't healed and trust isn't restored overnight. But in time, organizations, families and nations are changed by virtuous leaders. The good news is that men and women who act with patience, openness, tenderness, forgiveness, courage, gratitude, self-control and all other related virtues can make a powerful difference in the world.

The good news is also that these virtues can be cultivated. Gratitude can be developed. Self-control can be nurtured. Surrender can be learned. Some "virtuous" actions can be set in motion by strategic design.

Yes, it takes time—sometimes many years—to build character, but effective leadership flows from character. And, as we have seen throughout these 30 days, developing character is ultimately a spiritual journey.

The story of King David unfolds as a master class in the character of a great leader. The 14 virtues explored in this book over the past 30 days show an all-too-human monarch striving to honor God and serve his people with integrity.

It's the journey that our world, more than ever, needs us to take. It's a journey that can bless families, churches, organizations and nations. I hope that this book has been an inspiration and a companion for you on your own journey.

The God of justice is with us,

and our word, our work—

our prayer for freedom—

will not, cannot be in vain.

—Elizabeth Cady Stanton

About the Authors

King David of Israel is an enduringly charismatic figure. I first heard about young David's being chosen king and slaughtering the giant Goliath in Sunday School. I learned that "David and Goliath" was shorthand in our culture for any underdog's surprising victory. I got to see Michelangelo's statue as a young boy, first in an art book and later in person. I was fascinated at the virile figure he cut. I could only hope as a fledgling adult that I might be able to measure up to the manly poet-warrior that Michelangelo had sculpted.

Sad to say, my muscles never developed like David's. My poetry skills reached their peak with the B-minus I got in Creative Writing. My warrior vision was ended by the Selective Service System assigning me #336 in the draft lottery of 1971. But the Religious Studies department at my university was offering stimulating courses on war and peace, nonviolence, conscience and ethics as well as the Old and New Testaments. I got hooked. This teaching spoke to my mind, my heart and my spirit. I declared a Religious Studies major, joined my denominational campus ministry, decided to check out Yale Divinity School—and, in that process, heard God's clear call to ministry. Upon graduating from seminary, I was appointed to my first congregation, beginning a career of 42 years-and-counting of pastoral ministry.

In my work as a pastor and teacher, I've read many books on David, especially the ones that focused on his songs and his spirituality. He always seemed captivating and elusive, intriguing but mysterious.

This book had its genesis in a series of sermons I delivered as a pastor. You may know that pastors often choose their passages from a guide to scriptures called the Revised Common Lectionary. The lectionary is simply a three-year standardized list of Bible passages recommended for the focus of Sunday sermons, so that congregations get to hear the broad sweep of the Bible over those three years. During one summer of this three-year cycle there is a series of 11 consecutive passages on David. I decided to preach on these passages, calling the series "Leadership Lessons from King David."

Most of my ministry has been in the Washington, DC suburbs. Many parishioners in these churches hold high-level jobs in the military, government and consulting worlds. Leadership development is an ongoing professional need, and most folks have been what we'd call "high achievers" anyway. I assumed people would appreciate their church helping them in their work.

I later changed the title to "Leadership Secrets of King David." I thought that "Secrets" sounded more intriguing than "Lessons." People love to know secrets, so I was positive they'd flock to hear the "secrets" of leadership. Surely biblical perspectives on leadership would be enthralling material that might lead them toward raises and promotions at work. This compelling series would attract people far beyond our walls, overflow the pews and cause our summer attendance to skyrocket.

I'm sure you've guessed where this humbling story is headed. The sermon series did not electrify the community or pack the church—nor did it lead to promotions and raises for our congregants.

The more I reflected on these passages from scripture—then, began to preach about these stories and got feedback from the congregation—I was reminded of a basic truth about good preaching and teaching. At our best, we are not listing lessons to be learned like consultants at a conference. Sermons on the "5 Ways to Do This" or the "3 Secrets of a Happy Whatever" usually land on our hearts as burdens—guilt instead of grace. "Try more, add this, remember that, work harder, practice this and do better" is a cheap and stressful substitute for the gospel. The best Christian preaching and teaching embraces the saving work of God through Jesus Christ and trusts that, if we welcome God's nurturing presence, we will slowly but surely shape our character—our very being—in God's image.

That's ultimately one of the most important leadership lessons from the life of David: He never claims to be a self-made man. That idea is foreign to him. As God guides him through a lifetime of challenges, opportunities, risks, failures and successes, David grows as a human being and a leader. He nurtures God's presence within him.

We can do the same thing.

Perhaps if we place ourselves in the stories of David, ask questions, find parallels to today, and open ourselves to the wisdom and grace God gave David, each one of us can be as David was … a person after God's own heart.

That phrase is twice applied to David in the Scriptures, "a man after God's own heart." (1 Samuel 13:14 and Acts 13:22). I heard this expressed just yesterday, when a parishioner heard I was writing a book about David.

"David?! You know, I could never understand why David was 'a man after God's own heart,'" Ginny said. "Sleeping with Bathsheba, killing her husband, lying about it—he was such a sleazeball!"

I wish I had been quick enough to reply, "Exactly! That's why there's hope for you and me, too."

Knowing that God loves and blesses even sleazeballs gives me hope. I pray this small book might be just that—a gift of hope for you and me and even the sleazeballs of this world, which ultimately flows from the heart of God.

Care to learn more?

There are many excellent commentaries on 1 and 2 Samuel (the primary source for David's life), as well as numerous free-standing biographies of this complex man. Davidophiles will also value commentaries and studies of Psalms. Similarly, there are thousands of books on spiritual growth, character development and leadership skills. Here I will share a few favorites that helped give shape to this book.

On King David

Perhaps the most widely read and admired Old Testament scholar of today is Walter Brueggemann, named by Amazon as "the world's leading interpreter of the Old Testament." Now retired from full-time teaching at Columbia Theological Seminary (Decatur, Georgia), he continues to write and lecture prolifically with passion and insight. I believe his books are absolutely essential for anyone wanting to hear the Old Testament speak with depth and power.

Jonathan Kirsch's *King David* is a provocative and engaging account of David's life. Augmented by the nuances of Hebrew language and rabbinic Midrash, Kirsch offers a vivid understanding of David's story. His liberal use of Jewish scholars enriches a sometimes controversial examination of David's character. This is a great place to begin understanding David's complexity.

Frank Johnson, Bruce Birch and Eugene Peterson are also astute scholars who have authored well-regarded commentary series. Malcolm

Gladwell is not a biblical scholar but does deserve mention for his creative book that applies the David and Goliath story to movements in contemporary life. I find all of Gladwell's books to be delightful reading.

- Birch, Bruce, "The Books of Samuel: Introduction, Commentary and Reflection," *The New Interpreter's Bible*, vol. 2, Leander Keck, General Editor. Nashville: Abingdon Press, 1998, pp. 947-1383.

- Brueggemann, Walter, *David's Truth (In Israel's Imagination and Memory)*. Fortress Press, 1985.

- Brueggemann, Walter, *First and Second Samuel: Interpretation: A Bible Commentary for Teaching and Preaching*. Louisville, Kentucky: Westminster / John Knox Press, 1990.

- Brueggemann, Walter, et al., *Texts for Preaching (Year B)*. Louisville, Kentucky: Westminster / John Knox Press, 1993.

- Gladwell, Malcolm, *David and Goliath*. New York: Little, Brown and Company, 2013.

- Johnson, Frank, *First and Second Samuel (Basic Bible Commentary Series)*. Nashville: Abingdon Press, 1988.

- Kirsch, Jonathan, *King David: The Real Life of the Man Who Ruled Israel*. New York: Ballentine Books, 2000.

- Peterson, Eugene H., *First and Second Samuel (Westminster Bible Companion)*. Louisville, Kentucky: Westminster / John Knox Press, 1999.

On Spiritual Growth and Character

The books I suggest in this section are those that have been formative for me, so they reveal as much about this author as they do about the subjects themselves. Jim Harnish's book offered me a first look into how the life of David provides a model for developing character and spiritual richness. All of Harnish's books crackle with freshness, humanity, scholarship and warmth. Henri Nouwen and Bill Coffin are two people I was privileged to know in my years at Yale Divinity School. One was a quiet Catholic priest, born in the Netherlands and continually called to a ministry with the poor, who was gifted in relating the depths of his personal struggles to the great mercy of God. The other was an ebullient Protestant preacher with deep roots in American privilege whose activism and preaching fueled critical movements for peace and social justice. Nouwen (as well as poet Rainer Rilke) writes with an invitation for thoughtful reflection; Coffin's sermons inspire passionate action.

- Coffin, William Sloane, *The Collected Sermons of William Sloane Coffin, The Riverside Years,* 2 vols. Louisville, Ky: Westminster John Knox Press, 2008.
- Harnish, James A., *Passion, Power & Praise: A Model for Men's Spirituality from the Life of David.* Nashville: Abingdon Press, 1999.
- Nouwen, Henri J. M., *In the Name of Jesus: Reflections on Christian Leadership.* New York: Crossroad Publishing Company, 1989, 2002.
- Rilke, Rainer Maria, *Letters to a Young Poet,* Revised Edition. New York: W. W. Norton & Co., 1962.

On Leadership

Stephen Covey's material, first published over 20 years ago, may seem dated, but his books are classic works on character-building for leadership. There are other worthwhile books bearing the Covey name, but these two (plus a three-day workshop in Covey's basic approach) guided my thinking around the significance of mission and vision statements.

- Covey, Stephen, *The 7 Habits of Highly Effective People: Powerful Lessons in Personal Change.* New York: Simon and Schuster, 1989, 2004.
- Covey, Stephen, *The 7 Habits of Highly Effective Families.* New York: Golden Books, 1997.
- www.franklincovey.com

Rabbi Ed Friedman did pioneering work in applying the work of family psychiatrist Murray Bowen to organizations. Bowen's study of families led to his developing what has come to be known as Bowen Theory (or Bowen Family Systems Theory, or simply Family Systems Theory). Bowen and Friedman both focus on anxiety and how it's managed and used by leaders. I found the writings of Ed Friedman, as well as his student and colleague Roberta Gilbert, especially helpful for leading congregations during my ministry. They should be helpful to any leader, though they are addressed primarily to leaders of congregations.

- Friedman, Edwin H., *Generation to Generation: Family Process in Church and Synagogue.* New York: Guilford Press, 1985.
- Friedman, Edwin H., et al., *A Failure of Nerve: Leadership in the Age of the Quick Fix*, Revised Edition. New York: Church Publishing, 2017.
- Gilbert, Roberta, *The Cornerstone Concept (In Leadership, In Life).* Falls Church, VA: Leading Systems Press, 2008.
- Gilbert, Roberta, *The Eight Concepts of Bowen Theory.* Falls Church, VA: Leading Systems Press, 2013.
- www.thebowencenter.org.

Several organizational consultants and coaches have combined to train coaches and consultants in using Bowen's theory in business organizations. Their approach is "second-generation" work after Friedman, Gilbert and others, and they faithfully use the key Bowen concepts to diagnose organizational problems and develop less anxious leaders. Jeffrey Miller's book describes the daily life of a fictional organization in realistic terms.

- Duggan, Bob, and Moyer, Jim, *Resilient Leadership: Navigating the Hidden Chemistry of Organizations.* West Conshohocken, PA: Infinity Publishing, 2009.
- Duggan, Bob, and Theurer, Bridgette, *Resilient Leadership 2.0: Leading with Calm, Clarity, and Conviction in Anxious Times.* United States: (No publisher listed), 2017.
- www.resilientleadershipdevelopment.com
- Miller, Jeffrey A., *The Anxious Organization: Why Smart Companies Do Dumb Things.* Facts on Demand Press, 2008.

There is an overwhelming industry in books on leadership: the cursory entry "leadership" in Amazon alone yields over 40,000 results. It would be impossible (and probably useless) to keep up with everything written about leadership even in the first two decades of the 21st century. Ronald Heifetz's book dates from the closing years of the last century and uses many examples of political leadership. I drew on his writings on adaptive leadership to describe David's actions during Absalom's revolt. James Kouzes and John Maxwell offer recent and highly regarded insights on organizational leadership.

- Heifetz, Ronald A., *Leadership Without Easy Answers*. Cambridge, MA: Belknap Press, 1994.

- Kouzes, James M., and Posner, Barry Z., *Encouraging the Heart*. San Francisco: Jossey-Bass, 2003.

- Kouzes, James M., and Posner, Barry Z., *The Leadership Challenge: How to Make Extraordinary Things Happen in Organizations*, Fifth Edition, 25th Anniversary. San Francisco: Jossey-Bass, 2012.

- Kouzes, James M., and Posner, Barry Z., eds., *Christian Reflections on the Leadership Challenge*. San Francisco: Jossey-Bass, 2014.

- Maxwell, John, *Leadership 101: What Every Leader Needs to Know*. Nashville: Thomas Nelson Publishers, 2002.

Discussion Guide

America ranks as one of the most religious nations on earth in global studies of religion, and faith plays a prominent role in this country in relationships and moral choices. That's why this book opens with thoughtful introductions by two of our nation's veteran political leaders—one a Democrat and one a Republican, coming together to recommend a national conversation on this book. This discussion guide outlines next steps in sparking that kind of healthy dialogue. You won't have trouble finding willing friends. There already are millions of small groups across America that regularly meet in congregations, libraries and community centers. Whether in person or virtually, I hope your group will find some or all of these suggestions helpful.

You know your group better than I do, of course. So, choose whatever questions you think will best engage your friends. Sometimes fewer questions prepared in advance will allow space for participants to think deeply and formulate responses, and to interact more deeply with each other. In other cases, pointed questions spark the most spirited discussion.

The biggest question group leaders ask is: How much time should we set aside?

This book is perfectly designed for reflections ranging from the "Thirty Days" in the title—to more focused group discussions, even in a single session. In addition to the division into 30 days, this book examines a series of 14 events in David's life, connected to 14 contemporary virtues. There are many ways to divide this material for meaningful small-group interaction.

Single Session

There are questions already included in each of the 30 chapters in this book. However, a single gathering to talk about *Thirty Days with King David* calls for more general questions. The following examples could help shape your meeting to fit your particular purposes.

1. What expectations did you have about reading this book? Were they met or not?
2. Prior to reading this book, what initial impressions did you have about David as a leader?
3. What was the most significant event in David's life? What can our society today best learn from that?
4. Which Day and virtue spoke to you most powerfully?
5. Name one or two of the 14 virtues that seem most critically needed today. Why did you choose those?
6. What would you like to do differently in your own life as a result of this book?

Retreat Format

Because David is such a popular character with millions of people, an entire retreat can easily be built around his life using this book as a guide. Consider placing an advance group order of books for retreat participants (see our contact information below). Sessions and speakers can be chosen to relate to the sessions described later in this guide. There are examples of each virtue applied to families, congregations and organizations.

Four to Six Sessions

Many small groups connected with congregations like to plan short-term series that run less than two months. Here's one way to format that approach.

If you've distributed books before the first session and introductory material has been discussed in advance, a group may need only four sessions to follow the suggested model. However, many groups like to schedule an introductory session to hand out copies, collect payment and offer an overview of the book itself. New groups also will want to invite participants to introduce themselves and share their hopes for the group, possibly using suggestions from the "Single Session" questions above. Then, most groups will enjoy a final session to welcome discussion on unaddressed material, unfinished conversations, unasked questions, new insights and group closure.

Here are two different ways to divide the book for this time frame.

Option 1:

1. Introductory session
2. Themes of Patience, Vision, Humility
3. Integrity, Openness, Tenderness, Forgiveness
4. Courage, Gratitude, Self-Control, Surrender
5. Perseverance, Calmness, Justice
6. Closing session

Option 2:

1. Introductory session
2. David's Early Life – Parts 1 to 3
3. David's Adulthood – Parts 4 to 9
4. David's Crises – Parts 10 to 11
5. Winding Down – Parts 12 to 14
6. Closing Session

Fourteen or More Sessions

If your group really wants to dive into the life of David and his wisdom for leaders today, you could enjoy several months of weekly sessions by dividing the book into 14 virtues.

Or, you could even extend the discussions into a full 30 sessions. Imagine inviting a small group of friends to read these chapters daily with you across 30 days—and share insights each day via social media.

Explore the Text

Finally, most small groups connected with congregations enjoy approaching Bible study by bringing multiple English translations into the discussion. If this book becomes your first foray into Bible study, you will find many translations available for free online. The members of your group are likely to own various translations. These English renderings of the original Hebrew scriptures range from centuries-old English translations, such as the King James Version, with dramatic poetry that continues to echo throughout our popular culture—to contemporary paraphrases of the scriptures such as The Message that are designed to heighten the suspense and power of the story. Among the most popular versions in mainline churches—and highly respected for its accuracy—is the New Revised Standard Version, which is the translation excerpted in this book.

Learn More

Want to place a group order of books? Contact our publishing house at info@FrontEdgePublishing.com. If you are planning a larger "group read" of 100 or more individuals, ask our publishing house about personalizing that shipment of books for your organization. We could add your logo to the cover, for example.

Care to ask a question? Visit our online resource page at www.ThirtyDaysWith.com.

Got news to share? We would enjoy hearing about your community's experience with this book. Please, send us a summary of your experience and include photos if you have them. We often publish newsy updates from across the country in our Front Edge Publishing weekly columns and in our related www.ReadTheSpirit.com online magazine.

Acknowledgments

It's clearly taken me a lifetime to write this simple book. Among the thousands of people who've traveled with me to this point, I want to thank these people in particular:

The people of Monumental United Methodist Church, Portsmouth, Virginia, my childhood church home; Sunday School teachers, friends, pastors, and adults who served as church leaders, unaware that a young boy was watching and learning about ordinary human integrity and unique divine love; I was unaware of what I'd learned until years later.

Old Testament professors Harry Gamble, Brevard Childs, Steven Tuell, Bruce Birch and Walter Brueggemann, for the sheer passion and joy they radiate in their teaching the Hebrew Scriptures.

James Harnish, whose book on King David and men's spirituality prompted the formation of a church men's group that continues to this day, and for the rich conversations his writing sparked among us.

The people of Burke and Herndon United Methodist Churches in Virginia, for their love of the Bible and their consistent prayerful support.

Faculty and colleagues at Wesley Theological Seminary, Washington, D.C.

The late Rev. Bob Edgar, clergy colleague, congressman, seminary president, National Council of Churches president, and president of Common Cause (2007-2013), who inspired his pastor more than he knew, and whose pastor wishes Bob's insights could have enriched the book you're holding; it would have been much the better for it.

My wife Beverly, and our sons Garrett and Tyler, who've inspired and blessed me on countless occasions with their courage, forgiveness, tenderness, integrity and perseverance.

Visit www.ThirtyDaysWith.com and sign up to receive news about the *Thirty Days With* series.

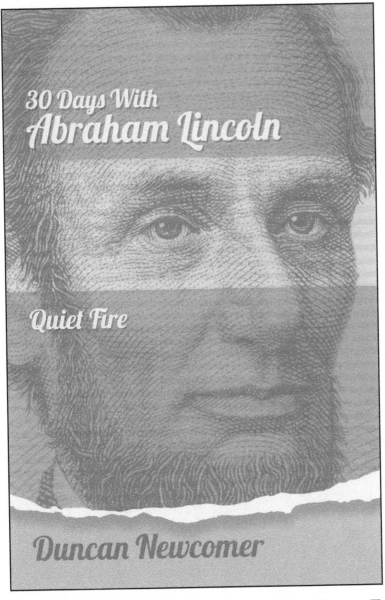

Thirty Days With Abraham Lincoln: Quiet Fire is available on Amazon.com and other online retailers.